The Wit and Satire of Bernard Shaw

The Wit and Satire of
Bernard Shaw

by Fred Mayne

Department of English, University of the Witwatersrand,
Johannesburg, South Africa

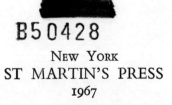

NEW YORK
ST MARTIN'S PRESS
1967

Library of Congress Catalog Card Number 67-14006

Printed in Great Britain by
Billing & Sons Limited, Guildford and London

Preface

BUFFON's dictum 'Le style est l'homme même' acquires particular significance when applied to the study of wit, which for an author may be either an intellectual stimulus or an emotional narcotic. Not that this book is a study of the man himself, human or Shavian. Discussion is confined almost entirely to the plays: in the context of Shaw's political and sociological onslaught on nineteenth and twentieth century England, the exercise of wit is isolated as a functional element in Shaw's dramatic production. His thought and personality are treated only in so far as they are revelant to techniques of wit. Quotations do not seek to provide empirical proof where none is possible, but to illustrate certain judgments and criteria, of which the validity can be tested only from a consideration of all Shaw's work. No rash attempt is made to formulate a complete theory of wit, only to show wit in action. Finally, with its insistence that plays are meant to be spoken, this work on Shaw's rhetoric of comedy may make a contribution to the study of dramatic method and to the application of practical criticism to the study of drama.

A study of 'wit' presents certain difficulties. Its literary *confrères* such as humour, satire, comedy, irony, and so on, are not mutually exclusive; and there is no generic term to embrace all the means by which laughter and kindred physiological disturbances are provoked. Consequently the categories cannot always be separated for purposes of discussion; and, in order to avoid clumsy or pedantic circumlocutions, analysis must resort to ill-defined and arbitrarily connotative terms. An attempt has been made to separate the inseparable, but the homogeneity of the subject matter may have caused, in transitions and repetitions, some blurring of analytic distinctions.

I wish to record my sincere thanks to Professor H. K. Girling of York University, Toronto, for his advice and encouragement.

Acknowledgements

THE Author and Publisher wish to acknowledge the kind permission given by The Public Trustee and The Society of Authors to reprint excerpts from the works of George Bernard Shaw.

Some of the material in this book has appeared in a different form in *English Studies in Africa*, University of the Witwaterstrand, and in *Southern Review*, University of Adelaide. Thanks are due to these journals for permission to reprint.

Contents

Abbreviations

THE plays of George Bernard Shaw: references are made to the titles of the plays, the acts, and the pagination in *The Complete Plays of Bernard Shaw*, Munksgaard, Copenhagen (by arrangement with Odhams Press, London), n.d.

Prefaces: The prefaces of George Bernard Shaw: references are made to the title of the play or novel and the pagination in *Prefaces by Bernard Shaw*, Constable, London, 1934.

Intelligent Woman's Guide:
> Bernard Shaw, *The Intelligent Woman's Guide to Socialism, Capitalism, Sovietism, and Fascism*, 2 vols., Penguin, London, 1937.

Sixteen Self Sketches:
> Bernard Shaw, *Sixteen Self Sketches*, Constable (standard edn.), London, 1949.

Bentley, *Shaw*:
> Eric Bentley, *Bernard Shaw*, Robert Hale, London, 1950.

Bergson:
> Henri Bergson, *Laughter, An Essay on the Meaning of the Comic*, Tr. C. Brereton and F. Rothwell, Macmillan, London, 1911.

Chesterton:
> G. K. Chesterton, *George Bernard Shaw* (1909, additional chapter, 1935), The Bodley Head, London, 1948.

Freud:
> Sigmund Freud, *Wit and its Relation to the Unconscious* (1905), Tr. A. A. Brill, Kegan Paul, Trench, Trubner, London, 1922.

Harris:
> Frank Harris, *Bernard Shaw*, Gollancz, London, 1949.

Joad, *Shaw*:
> C. E. M. Joad, *Shaw*, Gollancz, London, 1949.

Nicoll:
> Allardyce Nicoll, *An Introduction to Dramatic Theory*, Harrap, London, 1923.

Potter:
>Stephen Potter, *Sense of Humour*, Max Reinhardt, London, 1954.

Potts:
>L. J. Potts, *Comedy*, Hutchinson, London, 1948.

Wilson, *Triple Thinkers*:
>Edmund Wilson, 'Bernard Shaw at Eighty', *The Triple Thinkers, Twelve Essays on Literary Subjects*, John Lehmann, London, 1952.

Worcester:
>David Worcester, *The Art of Satire*, Harvard University Press, Cambridge (Massachusetts), 1940.

In the footnotes the practice of giving place of publication only for centres other than London has been followed throughout.

Laughter is primarily an art of the brain; it is intellectual, critical, destructive, unfeeling, hostile; it is divorced in its purest forms from emotion; it is a judgment or a comparison . . . these propositions are behind nearly all authoritative writing upon the function of laughter in comedy.

John Palmer.

The judgment which produces the comic contrast is wit. . . . Wit is nothing but a free play of ideas.

Karl Fischer.

. . . the witticism adheres to the mode of expression which clothes the thought.

Sigmund Freud.

Wit is the disguised priest who unites every couple . . . [it is] the skill to combine with surprising quickness many ideas, which through inner content and connections are foreign to one another.

Jean Paul Richter.

Wit is, in fact, the eloquence of indifference. . . . To be indifferent or sceptical, requires no effort; to be enthusiastic and earnest, requires a strong impulsive and collective power. Wit and humour (comparatively speaking, or taking the extremes to judge of the gradations by) appeal to our indolence, our weakness and insensibility.

William Hazlitt.

PART I

Sound

CHAPTER I

Consonance and Consequence

WHEN Middleton Murry called Samuel Butler and Bernard Shaw 'two modern and closely allied masters of plain prose'[1] he was decrying the purple patch and attacking the heresy that fine prose is poetic prose. Nevertheless the expression 'plain prose' if applied to Shaw is misleading or at best inadequate. Shaw did not write plain prose; he was a rhetorician in the original uncorrupted Isocratic and Aristotelian sense. He was, as Eric Bentley called him, 'a poet of polemics'.[2] He wrote to convert other people to his own opinions.

It was rhetoric that raised his non-dramatic writings far above the level of ordinary polemics and transformed chastening comedy into proselytizing satire. And it was this missionary zeal which prevented his rhetoric from lapsing into an artificial elegance, into the intellectual sterility with which its practice is so often associated. To say that he used rhetorical devices is merely to say that he was an artist or 'a poet of polemics' and not an expositor. To say that most of his rhetorical devices may be loosely classified under the heading of 'wit' is to say that he was concerned, among other things, with intellectual conversion. For Shaw meaning, not form, was important. Herbert Read's distinction between 'Elegance' as being concerned with the position of words and 'Wit' as being concerned with the meanings of words[3] is not entirely valid in that wit, too, has a secondary interest in the position and 'interanimation of words',[4] but it is valid in that wit is primarily intellectual in intention, if not in motivation.

Now it is not suggested that wit, any less than any other form of

---

[1] J. Middleton Murry, *The Problem of Style*, 1922, p. 67.
[2] Eric Bentley, *The Modern Theatre*, 1948, p. 98.
[3] Herbert Read, *English Prose Style*, 1928, p. 187.
[4] The term is borrowed from I. A. Richards, *The Philosophy of Rhetoric*, New York, 1936, Lecture III, p. 47.

rhetoric, cannot lead to a predominance of virtuosity over substance. It did with Oscar Wilde. At times it did with Shaw. But for Wilde, wit was a means of withdrawal, whereas for Shaw it was usually a means of attack and even more: it was a method of perception as well as of illumination. Particularly on the rhetorical level, his thought shaped his wit far more than his wit shaped his thought. He was primarily a witty writer and not a writer of witticisms:

DOOLITTLE. Dont say that, Governor. Dont look at it that way. What am I, Governors both? I ask you, what am I? I'm one of the undeserving poor: thats what I am. Think of what that means to a man. It means that he's up agen middle class morality all the time. If theres anything going, and I put in for a bit of it, it's always the same story: "Youre undeserving; so you cant have it." But my needs is as great as the most deserving widow's that ever got money out of six different charities in one week for the death of the same husband. I dont need less than a deserving man: I need more. I dont eat less hearty than him; and I drink a lot more. I want a bit of amusement, cause I'm a thinking man. I want cheerfulness and a song and a band when I feel low. Well, they charge me just the same for everything as they charge the deserving. What is middle class morality? Just an excuse for never giving me anything.

Pygmalion, Act II, pp. 729-30.

BENTLEY. . . . Then his mother was an Italian princess; and she had an Italian priest always about. He was supposed to take charge of her conscience; but from what I could make out she jolly well took charge of his. The whole three of them took charge of Joey's conscience. He used to hear them arguing like mad about everything. You see, the philosopher was a freethinker, and always believed the latest thing. The priest didnt believe anything, because it was sure to get him into trouble with someone or another. And the natural father kept an open mind and believed whatever paid him best.

Misalliance, p. 612.

In the first passage the wit infuses life into a straightforward analysis of charity that is conditional on conformity. In the second, it accentuates the subjectivity and self-interest at the root of certain patterns of belief. The dialogue is uncontrived and the wit is a product of perception rather than of artifice.

It was this almost complete fusion of wit and thought, with its consequent subordination of rhetorical figures, that ensured the integrity of Shaw's style and prompted Middleton Murry's 'plain prose' tribute. 'Dinna push, laddie, dinna push' is the soundest advice that can be given to any humorist, embryo or senescent. As critics have pointed out too often, 'inevitableness and surprise' is a criterion of good prose; and in wit, too, as this book tries to show, the element of surprise must be closely allied to an appearance of the inevitable. Sustained from below by a power, sincerity, and pertinacity of thought, Shaw's prose presents a surface which combines the pleasures of the expected with the stimulus of the unexpected.

Starting with the inevitable, the less obvious component of wit, my first task will be to show how he achieved this synthesis.

On a rhetorical level the appearance of the inevitable is achieved by an apparent ease of execution and speed of delivery. That Shaw's 'plain prose' was an excellent medium for polemics has already been remarked. Like Quintilian he did not believe that incomprehensibility was a sign of genius. Says Chesterton: 'The plain, pugnacious style of Shaw has greatly clarified all controversies. He has slain the polysyllable. . . . He does not think that difficult questions will be made simpler by using difficult words about them.'[5] In the twentieth century the slaying of the polysyllable is also a stylistic step in the achievement of a witty effect. The days of Dickens's unusual gymnastic and ablutionary performances or Sterne's hiatus in Phutatorius's breeches into which dropped the hot chestnut, are gone. We now think it funnier to be drunk than in an inebriated condition and funnier to be dead than to have crossed the Great Divide. If we were also certain that it is funnier to be polysyllabic than sesquipedalian, we might be tempted to represent a fashion as an immutable principle. But 'sesquipedalian' still has the virtue of the outlandish, and changes in style and wit are in great part mere changes in fashion, the outcome of the search for new, and therefore more potent, aesthetic stimuli. The terminological inexactitudes and exactitudes of polysyllabic humour represent an

[5] Chesterton, p. 243.

obsolescent phase, and it is enough to claim that twentieth-century taste prefers in wit a diction as simple as Shaw's.[6]

> SAVOYARD. Well, Vaughan has no sense of humor; and if you joke with him he'll think youre insulting him on purpose. Mind: it's not that he doesnt see a joke: he does; and it hurts him. A comedy scene makes him sore all over: he goes away black and blue, and pitches into the play for all he's worth.
>
> *Fanny's First Play*, Induction, p. 654.

This is, indeed, a far cry from the pompous prose of even the dialogue of the Shaw novels. But although some development towards humour may be discerned, the novels were comparatively humourless; and with Shaw the change in his style, already very evident in his dramatic and musical criticism, marks his evolution—almost revolution—into a wit.

Alliteration and assonance can be dealt with at the same time, for both serve a similar purpose. Both, by promoting speed of delivery and ease of apprehension, add to the feeling of the inevitable. Both, too, are inherently comic, embracing as they do the humour of Bergsonian automatism, and also its opposite pole, the sense of liberation—in this case from the trammels of language. Rhyme, too, is a form of assonance, and comic verse, with its over-emphatic, often far-fetched, rhyme and its pointed alliteration, as practised by Lewis Carroll, Edward Lear, and W. S. Gilbert—'I am the very model of a modern majorgeneral'—provides the most obvious literary field for its exploitation. Humorous literature, too, abounds in such names as Burglar Bill, Baby Bella, Ben Bluff, Willie Waugh, and Andrew Aguecheek. Is it not possible that the name of Charlie Chaplin, by some queer psychic alchemy, helped in some small degree to shape a career?

Alliteration and assonance are much more effective when the similarity of sound falls on the stressed syllables, ('with bloody, baleful blade'); and there seems little doubt that Shaw cast his sentences in this form in order to secure the maximum effect. That he used it as a conscious artifice is borne out by its abundance in the talk of his witty characters and its neglect in the responses of their foils.

[6] The modern American humorist, S. J. Perelman, successfully combines the polysyllabic with the outlandish, although he sometimes falls into laborious polysyllabic excess.

Tanner's contributions to his dialogue with the simple-minded Octavius and with the pompous Roebuck Ramsden, who as a comic but unwitty character is only alliterative in name, are given in evidence:

TANNER. .... She'll commit every crime a respectable woman can; and she'll justify every one of them by saying that it was the wish of her guardians. She'll put everything on us; and we shall have no more control over her than a couple of mice over a cat.

Man and Superman, Act I, p. 335.

TANNER. .... To women he is half vivisector, half vampire. He gets into intimate relations with them to study them, to strip the mask of convention from them, to surprise their inmost secrets, knowing that they have the power to rouse his deepest creative energies, to rescue him from his cold reason, to make him see visions and dream dreams, to inspire him, as he calls it.

Ibid., Act I, p. 341.

In the last quotation, alliteration is used to stress the key words 'study', 'strip', and 'surprise'. Such emphasis, which heightens both the contrast and similitude inherent in wit, is widely used by Shaw:

RICHARD. .... So I hear you are married, Pastor, and that your wife has a most ungodly allowance of good looks.

The Devil's Disciple, Act I, p. 225.

Often the witty effect produced by repetition is not gained by the repetition of the same sound but by *epizeuxis*—the repetition of the same word:

TANNER. That is the profoundest of mistakes, Tavy. It is the self-sacrificing women that sacrifice others most recklessly. Because they are unselfish, they are kind in little things. Because they have a purpose which is not their own purpose, but that of the whole universe, a man is nothing to them but an instrument of that purpose.

Man and Superman, Act I, p. 340.

TANNER (*seriously*). I know it, Ramsden. Yet even I cannot wholly

B

conquer shame. We live in an atmosphere of shame. We are ashamed of everything that is real about us; ashamed of ourselves, of our relatives, of our incomes, of our accents, of our opinions, of our experience, just as we are ashamed of our naked skins. Good Lord, my dear Ramsden, we are ashamed to walk, ashamed to ride in an omnibus, ashamed to hire a hansom instead of keeping a carriage, ashamed of keeping one horse instead of two and a groom-gardener instead of a coachman and footman. The more things a man is ashamed of, the more respectable he is. Why, youre ashamed to buy my book, ashamed to read it: the only thing youre not ashamed of is to judge me for it without having read it; and even that only means that youre ashamed to have heterodox opinions. Look at the effect I produce because my fairy godmother withheld from me this gift of shame.

Ibid., Act I, p. 337.

In the last quotation the word 'ashamed'—or 'shame'—is banged backwards and forwards like a tennis ball. The rally takes two or three shots to settle into a steady rhythm, varied by one or two lobs, and concludes with Tanner winding himself up and smashing home the winning shame in the last sentence.

When the alliteration or assonance would otherwise be too obvious to be a legitimate rhetorical aid, Shaw injects fresh humour by making fun of it, or by making it particularly appropriate to the character or the moment:

> ANN. Dont be foolish, Jack. Mr Ramsden has always been Grandpapa Roebuck to me: I am Granny's Annie; and he is Annie's Granny. I christened him so when I first learned to speak.
>
> *Ibid.*, pp. 338–9.

This, spoken in a very gentle voice, emphasises both the duplicity of Ann's pose of childlike and maidenly dependence and the fatuity of the fat-witted Roebuck Ramsden.

> SIR DEXTER. You come in the nick of time. Sir Jafna here has just been qualifying you as a bloodsucker, a pirate, a parasite, a robber baron and finally as vermin. Vermin! How do you like it?
>
> THE DUKE (*calmly taking the end chair nearest the window, on Basham's*

left). I wonder why the epithet robber is applied only to barons. You never hear of robber dukes; yet my people have done plenty of robbery in their time. (*With a sigh of regret*) Ah, thats all over now. The robbers have become the robbed.

On the Rocks, Act II, p. 1202.

The rhetorical emotionalism of Sir Jafna's romanticism and the urbane detachment of the Duke's realism are both underlined in this almost inconsequential, yet thematic reference to the 'robber baron'.

DON JUAN (*somewhat impatiently*). My point, you marble-headed old masterpiece, is only a step ahead of you. Are we agreed that life is a force which has made innumerable experiments in organizing itself; that the mammoth and the man, the mouse and the megatherium, the flies and the fleas and the Fathers of the Church, are all more or less successful attempts to build up that raw force into higher and higher individuals, the ideal individual being omnipotent, omniscient, infallible, and withal completely, unilludedly self-conscious: in short, a god?

. . . . . .

ANA. I most emphatically disagree as regards the Fathers of the Church; and I must beg you not to drag them into the argument.

DON JUAN. I did so purely for the sake of alliteration, Ana; and I shall make no further allusion to them.

Man and Superman, Act III, p. 379.

It was not, however, for the sake of alliteration for alliteration's sake, but for the sake of a satirically climactic contrast.

A last example, in which Mrs Pearce is asking Higgins not to use 'a certain word' which 'begins with the same letter as bath' in front of Eliza:

MRS. PEARCE. Only this morning, sir, you applied it to your boots, to the butter, and to the brown bread.

HIGGINS. Oh, that! Mere alliteration, Mrs Pearce, natural to the poet.

Pygmalion, Act II, p. 727.

It was also natural to a master of rhetoric. It sharpens the barb of his wit, and by assisting in the onrush of his prose heightens the feeling of the inevitable. Seldom does a lapse into 'apt alliteration's artful aid' produce a phrase as feeble as Tanner's 'Down with Government by the Greyhaired'.[7] Few writers are less likely than Shaw to trip up their readers by leaving their scaffolding lying around.

But the rapid flow of Shaw's prose is of course mainly achieved by assiduous attention to rhythm. Now, not all humorous writing requires a rapid tempo. Deprecatory humour and humour which depends on a simulated ingenuousness and earnestness may require a more halting rhythm, varied perhaps by little ridiculous rushes of confidence. The humour, too, which is combined with pathos must obviously suit the tempo to the mood. Polemical wit, however, must be delivered at great speed in order to preserve an appearance of confident objectivity and to promote that suspension of judgement so important to its success. The voluble and vivacious patter of Sullivan's music is the musical counterpart to, and the setting for, the satirical frivolity of Gilbert. Shaw not only provides a musical counterpart to his own wit, but also makes the most of the humour of the inevitable which is inherent in regular rhythm. It is not surprising that serious poetry with a too regular beat, so suitable for comic verse, easily slips into bathos and lends itself so well to parody.

Preceding and subsequent quotations so amply illustrate Shaw's rhetorical rhythm that perhaps the best way to show his fondness for it here is to quote abuses. So careful was Shaw to preserve the balanced flow of his sentences that he sometimes blunted the sharp edge of his thought and wit for this purpose:

> . . . and that people not subtle enough to accept its apparent paradoxes as valid statements of biological fact may be rhetorically described as intellectually damned.
>
> *Sixteen Self Sketches*, No. XIII, p. 73.

As a paradox is a truth which is only seemingly untrue, we must assume that an 'apparent paradox' is false and perhaps seemingly true, or is not a paradox at all. We must also assume that a statement of 'biological fact' is not necessarily valid. But apparently Shaw could not

[7] *Man and Superman*, Act I, p. 335.

resist the rhythmical—and alliterative—advantages to be gained by the insertion of 'apparent' and 'valid'. Furthermore, the use of the word 'rhetorically' in a rhetorical writer is almost laughably redundant. But 'rhetorically described' is required to achieve an alliterative and rhythmic balance with 'intellectually damned'.

> There is less harm in a well-fed lion. It has no ideals, no sect, no party, no nation, no class: in short, no reason for destroying anything it does not want to eat.
>
> *Ibid.*, No. VIII, p. 43.

The 'well-fed' is inconsistent with 'it does not want to eat'. A less euphonious and hungrier lion would have been a more accurate and more striking image. The omission of 'it does not want to eat' would, however, have ruined the balance of the sentence completely.

'Do not suppose for a moment,' said Shaw, 'that I learnt my art from English men of letters. True, they showed me how to handle English words; but if I had known no more than that, my works would never have crossed the Channel. My masters were the masters of a universal language; they were, to go from summit to summit, Bach, Handel, Haydn, Mozart, Beethoven and Wagner.'[8] It is significant that the final 'summit' is Wagner, whom Shaw described as 'the literary musican par excellence',[9] because his subject matter was so closely allied to his tone structures. For Shaw knew all about the dangers of rhythmical prose:

> HIGGINS. Pickering: this chap has a certain natural gift of rhetoric. Observe the rhythm of his native woodnotes wild. 'I'm willing to tell you: I'm wanting to tell you: I'm waiting to tell you.' Sentimental rhetoric! thats the Welsh strain in him. It also accounts for his mendacity and dishonesty.
>
> *Pygmalion*, Act II, p. 728.

The use of rhetorical rhythm was particularly dangerous for one who aimed at intellectual rather than emotional conversion. Rhythm exerts a hypnotic spell, evoking responses almost at a biological level. Nevertheless, as with alliteration and assonance, it is used far more freely in the speeches of his witty and proselytizing realists who give the

---

[8] Quoted by Wilson: *Triple Thinkers*, p. 173.
[9] 'The Perfect Wagnerite' (1898), *Major Critical Essays*, 1947, p. 266.

Shavian viewpoint than in the speech of the romantics; for self-expression naturally took the form of wit. Tanner's speeches are wittier and more rhythmical than Ramsden's or Octavius's, Don Juan's than the Statue's, Undershaft's than Stephen's, Magnus's than Boanerges's, and those of the realistic realist, Larry Doyle, than those of the romantic realist, Tom Broadbent. Characters representing the opposition seldom use the rhythmic rhetoric which is so often the vehicle for Shaw's satiric powers of persuasion:

STEPHEN (*springing up again*). I am sorry, sir, that you force me to forget the respect due to you as my father. I am an Englishman; and I will not hear the government of my country insulted. (*He thrusts his hands in his pockets, and walks angrily across to the window.*)

UNDERSHAFT (*with a touch of brutality*). The government of your country! *I* am the government of your country: I, and Lazarus. Do you suppose that you and half a dozen amateurs like you, sitting in a row in that foolish gabble shop, can govern Undershaft and Lazarus? No, my friend: you will do what pays us. You will make war when it suits us, and keep peace when it doesnt. You will find out that trade requires certain measures when we have decided on those measures. When I want anything to keep my dividends up, you will discover that my want is a national need. When other people want something to keep my dividends down, you will call out the police and military. And in return you shall have the support and applause of my newspapers, and the delight of imagining that you are a great statesman. Government of your country! Be off with you, my boy, and play with your caucuses and leading articles and historic parties and great leaders and burning questions and the rest of your toys. *I* am going back to my counting-house to pay the piper and call the tune.

STEPHEN (*actually smiling, and putting his hand on his father's shoulder with indulgent patronage*). Really, my dear father, it is impossible to be angry with you. You dont know how absurd all this sounds to me. You are very properly proud of having been industrious enough to make money; and it is greatly to your credit that you have made so much of it. But it has kept you in circles where you are valued for your money and deferred to for it, instead of in the doubtless very old-fashioned and behind-the-times public school and university where I formed my habits of mind. It is natural for you to think that money governs England; but you must allow me to think I know better.

Major Barbara, Act III, pp. 490–1.

With its 'proud of having been', its 'made so much of it', its 'instead of in', and its 'deferred to for it', Stephen's diligent misinterpretation stands in strong contrast to Undershaft's resonant rhetoric.

Not only does the style of speech suit the speaker, but it also varies widely in the same speaker. This does not mean that the characters necessarily speak out of character, but that they change under the pressure of a new situation or, as is more likely in Shaw, under the pressure of a new idea or challenge. The diffident Undershaft of the first Act is not the proselytizing Undershaft of the second and third Acts. Cusins, the detached and witty bystander of the beginning of the play, finally becomes Cusins, the convert. With these changes comes a change in the rhythm of their speeches. How out of character would have been the following rhetorical outburst from an unconverted Cusins:

> CUSINS. You cannot have power for good without having power for evil too. Even mother's milk nourishes murderers as well as heroes. This power which only tears men's bodies to pieces has never been so horribly abused as the intellectual power, the imaginative power, the poetic, religious power that can enslave men's souls. As a teacher of Greek I gave the intellectual man weapons against the common man. I now want to give the common man weapons against the intellectual man. I love the common people. I want to arm them against the lawyers, the doctors, the priests, the literary men, the professors, the artists, and the politicians, who, once in authority, are more disastrous and tyrannical than all the fools, rascals, and impostors. I want a power simple enough for common men to use, yet strong enough to force the intellectual oligarchy to use its genius for the general good.

> *Ibid.*, Act III, p. 502.

The wit is still there but it is now a wit informed by a more constructive purpose. It is the same kind of wit as that of the later Undershaft.

The more emphatic rhythm of the proselytizing realists is, of course, the vehicle for more effective assertion, for a rhetoric which, if broken into its elements, has the superficial appearance of invective. But it is raised far above the level of invective and declamation to high satire by the loftiness of the theme, by the intensity of moral feeling, and, what concerns us more at the moment, by the extraordinary skill with which the units of invective are built up into a glittering and imposing configuration. The rhythm contributes to the appearance of effortlessness and is the cement which binds the structure together. The result is what we may call an oratorical style.

Many discussions on Shaw's style recognise that it was shaped on the public platform, but forget that the stage is a public platform and that, stylistically, the distinguishing feature of written polemic is its oratorical form.

> Shaw had no patience with discussions concerning the niceties and secret subtleties of literary style. He insisted that in writing the one and only thing to aim at was effectiveness of assertion. . . . Shaw's most conspicuous fault was over-emphasis. It belonged to his method and was deliberately cultivated, and it is hard not to believe that the habit of it, a habit which grew, was largely born of the platform.[10]

Frank Harris called it 'harangue-writing'[11] and estimated that during his Socialist period Shaw gave a thousand harangues in twelve years.[12]

Now such criticism is hardly legitimate unless we expect, for instance, irony in advertisement copy or wit in an obituary notice. Shaw either wrote frank polemic or he wrote for the stage, and dramatic dialogue demands an immediate response from an audience. This response is conditioned by the volatility of the spoken word, and by participation as a member of a by no means homogeneous group. Of a secluded reader a much more active, and therefore, imaginative response should be sought by means of a more indirect and allusive style. A reading of Shaw may at times produce a feeling of being bludgeoned into acquiescence by a continuous and wearisome violence of assertion; but listening to him in the auditorium, this 'biting over-emphasis'[13] is effective in gaining unremitting attention to the spoken word. A similar feeling of fatigue and consequent decline in attention or mindfulness may

[10] S. K. Ratcliffe, 'Shaw as a Young Socialist', *Shaw and Society*, ed. C. E. M. Joad, 1953, pp. 63–4.
[11] Harris, p. 98.   [12] *Ibid.*, p. 93.
[13] Edmund Wilson, 'Bernard Shaw on the Training of a Statesman', *Classics and Commercials*, 1951, p. 240.

perhaps be brought on by reading through Shakespeare's flood of metaphor, particularly in the later plays; but Shakespeare's metaphor is less a poetic parallel than a corporeal substitute, and from the stage it is a marvellous means of bodying forth a complex situation. Even if Shaw, like Shakespeare, had not been careful to give his audiences a rest from his rhetorical fireworks, the sheer brilliance of the display would be almost enough to ensure unflagging attention.

As it is, the very rhythm by which he expressed vehemence is also an instrument for variety and relaxation:

> THE DEVIL. . . . . This marvellous force of Life of which you boast is a force of Death: Man measures his strength by his destructiveness. What is his religion? An excuse for hating me. What is his law? An excuse for hanging you. What is his morality? Gentility! an excuse for consuming without producing. What is his art? An excuse for gloating over pictures of slaughter. What are his politics? Either the worship of a despot because a despot can kill, or parliamentary cock-fighting.
>
> *Man and Superman*, Act III, p. 376.

The rhetorical questions supply a progressively upward swing. The 'excuse', made scornfully and satirically emphatic by repetition, marks the highest point in each sense group, after which there is a falling away. The exclamatory 'Gentility' marks the highest point of the aggregation. The definitive diminuendo is heralded by the omission of the 'excuse', and a derisive and expectorative 'cock-fighting' applies the closure.

> UNDERSHAFT. I want a man with no relations and no schooling: that is, a man who would be out of the running altogether if he were not a strong man. And I cant find him. Every blessed foundling nowadays is snapped up in his infancy by Barnardo homes, or School Board officers, or Boards of Guardians; and if he shews the least ability he is fastened on by schoolmasters; trained to win scholarships like a racehorse; crammed with secondhand ideas; drilled and disciplined in docility and what they call good taste; and lamed for life so that he is fit for nothing but teaching. If you want to keep the foundry in the family, you had better find an eligible foundling and marry him to Barbara.
>
> *Major Barbara*, Act III, p. 489.

Here there is less warmth than in the previous example. Consequently the crescendo is less marked and the passage free from the more vehement figures of *exclamation*, *interrogation*, and *epizeuxis*. The arrival at the summit is signalized by the explosive alliteration of 'drilled and disciplined in docility', and the descent by the falling alliteration of 'lamed for life'. At first sight it might be thought that the upward surge towards the summit would have been better achieved if the shorter 'crammed with secondhand ideas' had preceded the longer 'trained to win scholarships like a racehorse'. But as a composition in sound, the assonance and alliteration of 'crammed with secondhand ideas' provide a more effective approach to the alliterative climax; and as an essay in sense, the more comprehensive and, in this case, more important of the two phrases should be on a higher level than the other. Shaw uses the vehement rhetorical device of '*Incrementum*, the scaling ladder, which climbs to the top of high comparison'[14] very frequently and with a great technical skill.

Another figure greatly favoured by Shaw for increasing the force of assertion is that of *interrogation*, which 'serves where bare affirmation would be too gentle and harmless a speech.'[15] With Shaw its rising intonation becomes not only a means of vehemence but also a means of imparting rhythmical swing:

> SIR JAFNA. Your land monopolists. Your blackmailers. Your robber barons. Look at my Blayport Docks reconstruction scheme! Am I a public benefactor or am I not? Have I not enough to live on and die on without troubling myself about Blayport? Shall I be any the happier when it has ten square miles of docks instead of a tuppenny-hapeny fishing harbor? What have I to gain except the satisfaction of seeing a big publicly useful thing well done, and the knowledge that without me it could not be done? Shall I not be half ruined if it fails?
>
> *On the Rocks*, Act II, pp. 1201–2.

There is sufficient emotional heat to make simple affirmation inadequate. Exclamatory assertions, nearly always associated with a loud voice, are, however, alien to the spirit of wit. Consequently, it falls to interrogation to provide emphasis, stress without strain.

[14] Rosemond Tuve, *Elizabethan and Metaphysical Imagery*, Chicago, 1947, p. 188.
[15] *Ibid.*, p. 188.

Exclamation, indeed, is seldom used in the ordinary fashion by Shaw to express 'extremity of "motion" '.[16] More often it serves to prevent the dialogue from flagging. As in these extracts from *Caesar and Cleopatra*, it is used frequently at the beginning of speeches to provide an emphatic link with the words of the previous speaker:

> CAESAR (*calmly*). Well, my friend; and is not this very natural?
> POTHINUS (*astonished*). Natural! Then you do not resent treachery?
> CAESAR. Resent! O thou foolish . . .
>
> *Caesar and Cleopatra*. Act IV, p. 287.

> CAESAR (*affectionately*). No, my son Rufio, but to please me—to celebrate my birthday.
> RUFIO (*contemptuously*). Your birthday! You always have a birthday when there is a pretty girl to be flattered or an ambassador to be conciliated. We had seven of them in ten months last year.
> CAESAR (*contritely*). It is true, Rufio! I shall never break myself of these petty deceits.
> RUFIO. Who is to dine with us—besides Cleopatra?
> CAESAR. Apollodorus the Sicilian.
> RUFIO. That popinjay!
> CAESAR. Come! the popinjay is an amusing . . .
>
> *Ibid.*, Act IV, p. 285.

The exclamatory repetitions express no stronger emotions than those of impatience, surprise, and mild contempt.

Seldom, however, does Shaw use *exclamation* at the beginning of a long speech which is to work up to a climax. Shaw was too able a rhetorician to anticipate a climax and too good a writer to have need of such an obvious device as *exclamation* for expressing 'extremity of "motion" '.

The extracts illustrating *exclamation* provide further examples of *epizeuxis*. Its additional potentialities for producing a humorous effect by repetition make it a favourite figure with Shaw for promoting vehemence. It has already been treated as a specialised form of assonance, and further examples will be found in subsequent extracts. One last example in a different strain will be enough:

---

[16] *Ibid.*, p. 188.

VALENTINE. Of course not. Now what happens in the duel of sex? The old fashioned daughter received an old fashioned education to protect her against the wiles of man. Well, you know the result: the old fashioned man got round her. The old fashioned mother resolved to protect her daughter more effectually—to find some armor too strong for the old fashioned man. So she gave her daughter a scientific education: your plan. That was a corker for the old fashioned man: he thought it unfair, and tried to howl it down as unwomanly and all the rest of it. But that didnt do him any good. So he had to give up his old fashioned plan of attack: you know: going down on his knees and swearing to love, honor, and obey and so on.

You Never Can Tell, Act III, p. 202.

In this extract a humorous rather than a hortatory effect predominates. The repetitive 'old fashioned' is not banged rhythmically and vehemently to and fro as in the previously quoted 'ashamed' speech of Tanner[17] and the 'excuse' speech of the Devil.[18] Its reappearances are inevitable but desultory, and do not form a framework around which the passage is built. Indeed, the passage has no structure, if by structure is meant some measure of periodicity or some appearance of balance. It jolts along, banging on all buffers and spluttering to the appropriately inconclusive conclusion of 'and so on'. But it is this looseness of form which is so friendly to comedic as opposed to polemical wit. For although solemnity of structure may add polish to the irony of a Gibbon, it is alien to dialogue, to Shaw's breezy and oratorical polemic, and to his bubbling wit. Even in his polemical wit the periodicity, so necessary for didactic emphasis, is what might be called a rhythmic periodicity, achieved mainly through the careful balance and articulation of grammatically loose components both within and without the limits of the sentence. Indeed, although the single periodic sentence is likely to be more rhythmical than a loose sentence, the very fact that it is itself a rhythmic unit makes it more difficult to fit into a more sustained rhythmic pattern, whether the pattern be climactic or not:

THE ELDERLY GENTLEMAN (*nobly*). My body is dust, madam: not my soul. What does it matter what my body is made of? the dust of the ground, the particles of the air, or even the slime of the

[17] See pp. 7–8.   [18] See p. 15.

ditch? The important thing is that when my Creator took it, whatever it was, He breathed into its nostrils the breath of life; and Man
became a living soul. Yes, madam, a living soul. I am not the dust of
the ground: I am a living soul. That is an exalting, a magnificent
thought. It is also a great scientific fact. I am not interested in the
chemicals and the microbes: I leave them to the chumps and noodles,
to the blockheads and the muckrakers who are incapable of their
own glorious destiny, and unconscious of their own divinity. They
tell me there are leucocytes in my blood, and sodium and carbon
in my flesh. I thank them for the information, and tell them that
there are black beetles in my kitchen, washing soda in my laundry,
and coal in my cellar. I do not deny their existence; but I keep them
in their proper place, which is not, if I may be allowed to use an
antiquated form of expression, the temple of the Holy Ghost. No
doubt you think me behind the times; but I rejoice in my enlighten-
ment; and I recoil from your ignorance, your blindness, your im-
becility. Humanly I pity you. Intellectually I despise you.

Back to Methuselah, Part IV, Act I, p. 918.

It is not only the sense, but the rhythm, that bears the reader along on
successive waves. It is the rhythm, not only the sense, that imparts the
feeling of inevitability which turns each loose unit into an integral
part of a periodic whole. It would be reading our knowledge of the
completed passage into the consideration of a fragment if we said that
we could not stop anywhere but at the end without a feeling of frustration or loss; but nevertheless we can fairly say that at no point is there
any sense of discontinuity or even discontinuance, except possibly between 'divinity' and 'They tell me'. At no point, either, are difficult
transitions clogged up with grating and burdensome conjunctions,
which 'Of all the parts of speech,' wrote George Campbell, '. . . are
the most unfriendly to vivacity'.[19]

In polemical wit, then, the polemic is sustained by the rhythm of the
whole, and the wit finds free play in the looseness of the parts. In
comedic wit, however, which is practised more for its own sake, the
rhythm drops into the background; for Shaw seldom made the mistake of describing simple things in Olympian tones and terms. Language is always appropriate, and there is far less rhythmic rhetoric in the

---

[19] *Philosophy of Rhetoric* (1808), iii, 3; quoted by Herbert Read, *English Prose Style*, 1928, p. 54.

lighter comedies such as *Arms and the Man, The Philanderer, You Never Can Tell*, and *Pygmalion*. Where the matter is on a lower sociological plane, and the wit is an intellectual exercise, not serving an urgent moral necessity, Shaw gives full rein to his comedic talent, the loose sentences or units being given their head to wander where they please, both themselves and the reader; for, while polemical wit has a destination determined by the sense and guided by the rhythm, comedic wit meanders inconsequentially by the wayside.

THE COUNTESS. Excitement: thats what I get out of it. Look at Popsy and me! We're always planning robberies. Of course I know it's mostly imagination; but the fun is in the planning and the expectation. Even if we did them and were caught, there would be the excitement of being tried and being in all the papers. Look at poor Harry Smiler that murdered the cop in Croydon! When he came and told us what he'd done Popsy offered to go out and get him some cyanide to poison himself; for it was a dead sure thing that he'd be caught and bumped off. 'What!' says Harry; 'and lose the excitement of being tried for my life! I'd rather be hanged' he says; and hanged he was. And I say it must have been almost worth it. After all, he'd have died anyhow: perhaps of something really painful. Harry wasnt a bad man really; but he couldnt bear dullness. He had a wonderful collection of pistols that he had begun as a boy: he picked up a lot in the war. Just for the romance of it, you know: he meant no harm. But he'd never shot anyone with them; and at last the temptation was too great and he went out and shot the cop. Just for nothing but the feeling that he'd fired the thing off and done somebody in with it. When Popsy asked him why he'd done it, all he could say was that it was a sort of fulfilment. But it gives you an idea, doesnt it, of what I mean?

Too True to be Good, Act II, p. 1149.

As in Valentine's speech[20] on old-fashioned sex, the feeling of inevitability is still there in these rambling remarks on Harry's fate, but it is now no longer promoted by rhythm but by loose construction, which turns much of the passage into a series of apparently unpremeditated afterthoughts, and is as necessary for the humour of understate-

[20] See p. 18.

ment as is rhythmic emphasis for polemical wit. Murder most foul is discussed as a paltry peccadillo.

But along with the growing looseness of construction the element of surprise, which of course can never be entirely absent, has become more and more obtrusive. In other words, we are crossing over from the wit of euphony and consonance to the wit of dissonance in the realm of sound, and incongruity in the realm of ideas. For purposes of analysis we are still in the realm of sound, although in practice it is not possible to isolate completely the one from the other.

CHAPTER II

Dissonance and Consequence

THE pleasures of consonance are the pleasures of the expected and induce a feeling of content, relaxation, and receptivity. The pleasures of dissonance are the pleasures arising from the stimulus of the unexpected, and the resolution of the tension thus evoked. In the field of wit this resolution of tension will be accompanied by anything from a brightening of the eyes to a belly-laugh, according to the pitch of the tension and the speed and completeness of the resolution.[1] Incongruity of ideas may play a greater part in producing the more violent manifestations of amusement, but the incongruity will be lost without the skilful juxtaposition which is dependent on sound and timing; for by regulating the quality and even the quantity of the sound, timing is much more than a mere auxiliary.

The most obvious form of dissonance is frank and palpable anticlimax, a device for which Shaw is famous and notorious; and to which he is self-confessedly addicted:[2]

UNDERSHAFT. I dont. They do. You see, the one thing Jones wont stand is any rebellion from the man under him, or any assertion of social equality between the wife of the man with 4 shillings a week less than himself, and Mrs Jones! Of course they all rebel against me, theoretically. Practically, every man of them keeps the man just below him in his place. I never meddle with them. I never bully them. I dont even bully Lazarus. I say that certain things are to be done; but I dont order anybody to do them. I dont say, mind you, that there is no ordering about and snubbing and even bullying. The men snub the boys and order them about; the carmen snub the sweepers; the artisans snub the unskilled labourers; the foremen drive

---

[1] See pp. 41–2 for a brief discussion of wit as 'deceived expectation'.
[2] *Sixteen Self Sketches*, No. IX, p. 48.

and bully both the laborers and the artisans; the assistant engineers find fault with the foremen; the chief engineers drop on the assistants; the departmental managers worry the chiefs; and the clerks have tall hats and hymnbooks and keep up the social tone by refusing to associate on equal terms with anybody. The result is a colossal profit, which comes to me.

Major Barbara, Act III, p. 492.

Effective anticlimax is made easier in Shaw's dialogue through his habit of increasing the speed of his sentences by making the later parts longer than the earlier parts, and thus creating an overbalance. Contrast the shortness of the anticlimactic sentence 'The result is a colossal profit, which comes to me', with the length of the climactic items which it follows, and particularly with the length of the protracted concluding item, 'and the clerks have tall hats and hymnbooks and keep up the social tone by refusing to associate on equal terms with anybody'. The real anticlimax, however, is saved for one word at the end—'me', which, in its monosyllabic and egoistic brevity, provides a delicious contrast to the long list of self-important employees all quarrelling over a bone which the little 'me' is quietly eating in the corner. Some of the effect of this particular anticlimax may perhaps be lost because of previous amusement over the antics of the employees; but but with an actor to make an almost imperceptible pause before the 'me' it should earn a laugh from an audience, which, at this stage of the play, are convinced armament manufacturers or at least pro-Undershaft. Shorten or lengthen the anticlimactic sentence and the laugh would be less hearty.

THE BURGLAR. Simply enough. In her lily hand was a copy of The Lady's Pictorial. It contained an illustrated account of your jewels. Can you guess what Sweetie said to me as she gazed at the soft majesty of the mountains and bathed her soul in the beauty of the sunset?

THE PATIENT. Yes. She said 'Popsy: we must pinch that necklace.'

THE BURGLAR. Exactly. Word for word. But now can you guess what *I* said?

THE PATIENT. I suppose you said 'Right you are, Sweetie' or something vulgar like that.

c

THE BURGLAR. Wrong. I said, 'If that girl had any sense she'd steal the necklace herself.'

Too True to be Good, Act I, p. 1139.

The anticlimax is purely comedic and has no polemical overtones. The preliminary pause is taken up by the words 'Yes. She said 'Popsy: we must'' being lengthened by a colon after 'Popsy', where a comma would have been more grammatically usual. The pause after 'Popsy' is crucial, and there is no punctuation after 'She said', for Shaw knew that three pauses—there is another after 'Yes'—would make the interval between climax and anticlimax too long and too studied. That this is not just a punctuational vagary is shown by the insertion of a comma after the 'said' in the Burglar's third speech when Shaw needed a pause before what might be called an anti anticlimax. In the Patient's second speech, however, a comma after the 'said' is again not necessary, for the 'I suppose you said' is a long enough pause for an anticlimax which cannot hope to be very funny; and what is more, as the immediate repetition of exactly the same device lessens the humorous effect, provides a necessary variety in the type of pause used. The 'something vulgar like that' is the pause before the 'Wrong', and like many similar pauses provides the punch words with an island of greater audibility, which is particularly necessary if the previous words have aroused a laugh or a chuckle. The whole exchange shows how sensitive Shaw was to the effect of sound and timing on wit and the extraordinary care he put into the minutiae of his craft.

RAINA (*rising in indignant protest*). And so he becomes a creature incapable of faith and gratitude.

BLUNTSCHLI (*making a wry face*). Do you like gratitude? I dont. If pity is akin to love, gratitude is akin to the other thing.

RAINA. Gratitude! (*Turning on him.*) If you are incapable of gratitude you are incapable of any noble sentiment. Even animals are grateful. Oh, I see now exactly what you think of me! You were not surprised to hear me lie. To you it was something I probably did every day! every hour!! That is how men think of women. (*She paces the room tragically.*)

BLUNTSCHLI (*dubiously*). Theres reason in everything. You said youd told only two lies in your whole life. Dear young lady: isnt that rather a short allowance? I'm quite a straightforward man myself; but it wouldnt last me a whole morning.

RAINA (*staring haughtily at him*). Do you know, sir, that you are insulting me?

BLUNTSCHLI. I cant help it. When you strike that noble attitude and speak in that thrilling voice, I admire you; but I find it impossible to believe a single word you say.

RAINA (*superbly*). Captain Bluntschli!

BLUNTSCHLI (*unmoved*). Yes?

RAINA (*standing over him, as if she could not believe her senses*). Do you mean what you said just now? Do you know what you said just now?

BLUNTSCHLI. I do.

RAINA (*gasping*). I! I!!! (*She points to herself incredulously, meaning 'I, Raina Petkoff, tell lies!' He meets her gaze unflinchingly. She suddenly sits down beside him, and adds, with a complete change of manner from the heroic to a babyish familiarity.*) How did you find me out?

Arms and the Man, Act III, p. 113.

'How did you find me out' is not only the anticlimax of the passage but also the climax of the whole play. Consequently, Shaw isolates it with great care and elaboration. Bluntschli remains calmly seated while Raina rises 'in indignant protest', keeps her indignant tempo on the boil by pacing tragically up and down, and finally towers threateningly above him in preparation for the final collapse, which is physical as well as mental. As the climactic indignation approaches its highest point in 'I! I!!!', care is taken to ensure its rapid ascent by making Bluntschli's last contributions so short that they become merely accelerative provocations. The final preliminary before the monosyllabically prosaic anticlimax is, of course, non-verbal, consisting of the sitting down and the change in manner.

But there is in this passage another more essential and more bred in the bone anticlimactic form. The shock of dissonance may provoke the heartier laugh; but the prolonged discordance, which arises from the contrast between the thrilling exclamatory and interrogatory rhetoric of Raina, the romanticist, and the flat tones of Bluntschli, the realist, will bring a more prolonged amusement in its train. It is the classical comic situation of the Alazon being slowly mined from without by the Eiron until he suddenly collapses. The same process is continually at work in *Captain Brassbound's Conversion*:

Brassbound walks up and down the room, nursing his indignation. In doing so he unconsciously enters upon an unequal contest with Lady Cicely, who sits quietly stitching. It soon becomes clear that a tranquil woman can go on sewing longer than an angry man can go on fuming. Further, it begins to dawn on Brassbound's wrath-blurred perception that Lady Cicely has at some unnoticed stage in the proceedings finished Marzo's bandage, and is now stitching a coat. He stops: glances at his shirtsleeves; finally realizes the situation.

BRASSBOUND. What are you doing there, madam?

LADY CICELY. Mending your coat, Captain Brassbound.

BRASSBOUND. I have no recollection of asking you to take that trouble.

LADY CICELY. No: I dont suppose you even knew it was torn. Some men are born untidy. You cannot very well receive Sidi el—what's his name?—with your sleeve half out.

BRASSBOUND (*disconcerted*). I—I dont know how it got torn.

LADY CICELY. You should not get virtuously indignant with people. It bursts clothes more than anything else, Mr Hallam.

BRASSBOUND (*flushing quickly*). I beg you will not call me Mr Hallam. I hate the name.

. . . . . .

LADY CICELY (*returning to the tailoring question as if her last remarks were of no consequence whatever*). Did this sleeve catch you at all under the arm? Perhaps I had better make it a little easier for you.

BRASSBOUND (*irritably*). Let my coat alone. It will do very well as it is. Put it down.

LADY CICELY. Oh, dont ask me to sit doing nothing. It bores me so.

BRASSBOUND. In Heaven's name then, do what you like! Only dont worry me with it.

LADY CICELY. I'm so sorry. All the Hallams are irritable.

BRASSBOUND (*penning up his fury with difficulty*). As I have already said, that remark has no application to me.

LADY CICELY (*resuming her stitching*). Thats so funny! They all hate to be told that they are like one another.

BRASSBOUND (*with the beginnings of despair in his voice*). Why did you come here? My trap was laid for him, not for you. Do you know the danger you are in?

LADY CICELY. Theres always a danger of something or other. Do you think it's worth bothering about.

BRASSBOUND (*scolding her*). Do I think! Do you think my coat's worth mending?

LADY CICELY (*prosaically*). Oh yes: it's not so far gone as that.

BRASSBOUND. Have you any feeling? Or are you a fool?

LADY CICELY. I'm afraid I'm a dreadful fool. But I cant help it. I was made so, I suppose.

Captain Brassbound's Conversion, Act II, pp. 314–15.

In this justly famous comic scene the essential discordance between Lady Cicely and Brassbound is the same as that between Raina and Bluntschli, except that Captain Brassbound's irascibly staccato exclamations replace the thrilling tones of Raina. The stage directions emphasise the restlessness of the virtuous romanticist and the repose of the realist, who is now engaged on soothing and prosaic but very usfeul work on his behalf. Even the Eiron's affectation of stupidity is there, and Brassbound's fury is maintained by successive pricks until later on in the scene there is a sudden collapse on to a chair with a 'Damn you! you have belittled my whole life to me'.[3]

The difference between Tanner and Bluntschli, between Lady Cicely and the later Undershaft, is now clear. They are all realists; but Undershaft and Tanner are mainly engaged in converting to realism, Lady Cicely and Bluntschli in converting from romanticism. It is a process of inflation as opposed to one of deflation, and swelling rhetoric makes way for puncturing prods and probes. That all his characters talk alike all the time is one of the more ridiculous errors of anti-Shaviana. Manipulation of language as well as ideas is essential to wit.

The connection between loose construction and anticlimax is also clear. Loose construction is favourable to understatement, and rhythmically periodicised construction is favourable to didactic emphasis and overstatement. All understatement is anticlimactic, but ordinary understatement is anticlimactic only in relation to the situation it describes; whereas specific anticlimax is understatement, not only in

---

[3] *Captain Brassbound's Conversion*, Act II, p. 316.

relation to the situation it describes, but also by virtue of its position immediately after a climactic overstatement; and it is loose because it does not form part of the preceding periodic pattern. Consequently, specific anticlimax is usually more explosively laughable than ordinary understatement, providing, as it does, a sudden release from tension; for not only does polemical rhetoric with its facile speed afford a relaxation from the trammels of ordinary language, it also imposes restrictions of a different kind on free expression. Furthermore, as specific anticlimax lurks in all witticisms, it is itself more of a witticism than a mere link in a chain of witty writing.

The distinction between witticisms and witty writing is difficult to maintain and one that is only attempted in the interests of analysis; for specifically anticlimactic effects, as opposed to specific anticlimaxes, can be seen in witty writing which contains no obvious witticisms.[4] But perhaps the best way to demonstrate a distinction is to make a brief examination of the intermediary stages:

> LINA. No: that is popular low-class business. In our family we touch nothing but classical work. Anybody can do lamps and hat-stands. *I* can do silver bullets. That is really hard.
>
> *Misalliance*, p. 624.

Each of the last four sentences is shorter than the previous one, and this anticlimactic effect is witty because, as the sentences become shorter, Lina's long-bow becomes longer. The anticlimactic sound structure enhances the climactic effect of ideas, but there is no anti-climax and no witticism.

> TARLETON. Good. Well, do you like me? Dont misunderstand me: I'm perfectly aware that youre not going to fall in love at first sight with a ridiculous old shopkeeper. I cant help that ridiculous old shopkeeper. I have to carry him about with me whether I like it or not. I have to pay for his clothes, though I hate the cut of them:

---

[4] Arthur Koestler distinguishes between witticisms and witty writing in terms of 'bisociation'. A witticism or joke is the outcome of a collision between two ideas or streams of thought which normally move on two different planes, whereas witty writing or sustained humour is a 'series of minor explosions' which take place along the line of intersection between these two planes. See *The Act of Creation*, 1964, particularly p. 37, or *Insight and Outlook*, 1949, particularly pp. 95–6.

especially the waistcoat. I have to look at him in the glass while I'm shaving. I loathe him because he's a living lie. My soul's not like that: it's like yours. I want to make a fool of myself. About you. Will you let me?

Ibid., p. 625.

Again the sentences become more or less progressively shorter as Tarleton becomes more humorously specific. The longer 'Will you let me?' is a weakness as we read, but in the acting a laugh would almost certainly intervene after 'About you'. Again, then, no anticlimax and no witticism.

TARLETON. Stacks of em. Theres the family Bible, and the Doré Bible, and the parallel revised version Bible, and the Doves Press Bible, and Johnny's Bible and Bobby's Bible and Patsy's Bible and the Chickabiddy's Bible and my Bible; and I daresay the servants could raise a few more between them. Let her have the lot.

Ibid., p. 624.

'Let her have the lot' rounds off the paragraph neatly and wittily without being quite an anticlimax.

THE MAN. . . . You can always tell an old soldier by the inside of his holsters and cartridge boxes. The young ones carry pistols and cartridges: the old ones, grub.

Arms and the Man, Act I, p. 97.

Again, in effect, three sentences of declining length. But because of the earthy sound and earthy associations of the 'grub', and because of the more obviously anticlimactic construction we are on the boundaries of witticism, which depends not only on the 'swift juxtaposition of two ideas fundamentally inharmonious'[5] but also on the swift juxtaposition of two sounds fundamentally inharmonious.

MENDOZA (*advancing between Violet and Tanner*). Sir: there are two tragedies in life. One is to lose your heart's desire. The other is to gain it.

Man and Superman, Act IV, p. 404.

[5] Nicoll, p. 48.

We are now in the realm of witticism. The "collision"[6] is a major one; for, although in a less condensed form than is usual, this is undisguised paradox. And perhaps because of their anticlimactic structure, Shaw's witticisms run mainly to the word play, thought play, and reversal of the customary found in paradox and epigram.

And loose construction is naturally more common because it lends itself more easily, not only to anticlimax, but also to condensation that assists in the creation of the comic shock in a witticism; for omissions which make for condensation are much easier to make between the comparatively isolated components of loose construction.[7] Says Freud: 'Finally *omission*, which is comparable to condensation without substitutive formation, is also a form of allusion. For in every allusion there is really something omitted, namely, the trend of thought that leads to the allusion.'[8] It is, of course, the omission of the intervening trend of thought that increases the comic shock by bringing the discordant elements closer together. Looseness promotes the tightness that comes from condensation:

> THE BISHOP. . . . What God hath joined together no man ever shall put asunder: God will take care of that.
>
> *Getting Married*, p. 556.

> THE DEVIL. . . . for Englishmen never will be slaves: they are free to do whatever the Government and public opinion allow them to do.
>
> *Man and Superman*, Act III, p. 373.

These remarks are witticisms and not pontifications because man's vainglory is implied and not stated. The colon and the anticlimactic looseness make provision for the omission of the trend of thought.

> THE GENTLEMAN. . . . As a matter of fact, the sound of English makes me feel at home; and I dislike feeling at home when I am abroad.
>
> *Widowers' Houses*, Act I, p. 3.

---

[6] See footnote, p. 28.

[7] Perhaps the most famous epigram in the English language, 'Advice to those about to marry. Don't', is aggressively loose and anticlimactic.

[8] Freud, p. 107.

Condensation is here the outcome of word play, the 'at home' being used figuratively in the first part, and literally in the second part of the sentence.

> AUBREY (*straightening himself up to declaim*). Have I not told you that he is an atheist, and like all atheists, an inflexible moralist?
>
> *Too True to be Good*, Act II, p. 1146.

It is interesting to note that Shaw does not use his customary colon or semi-colon after 'atheist', presumably because the longer pause should take place after 'atheists', where a very extensive train of thought is omitted but where even a semicolon is punctuationally impossible. Aubrey's description of his father would not be a paradox but a mere mystification, unless it is agreed that in a conformist society a thinking heterodoxy is likely to be more truly religious or moral than an unthinking orthodoxy.

> TROTTER. . . . Half the young ladies in London spend their evenings making their father take them to plays that are not fit for elderly people to see.
>
> *Fanny's First Play*, Induction, p. 655.

The omission is contained in the idea that, as the older generation is more easily shocked, they should be more carefully protected. The structure is less loose than in the preceding examples, and affords a convenient transition to the more usual form of condensation associated with epigram and paradox, which are more often grammatically simple sentences and by reason of their very brevity cannot be loose in form. Nevertheless, they are still loose in essence and are still anti-climactic in form in so far as the epigrammatic or paradoxical nub is saved for the last word or words.

> The golden rule is that there are no golden rules.
>
> *Man and Superman*, Prefaces, p. 188.

The trend of thought omitted is so extensive that the outcome is not merely a paradox but a logical, though not cognitive, absurdity.

> BURGOYNE. . . . Take it quietly, Major Swindon: your friend the

British soldier can stand up to anything except the British War
Office.

> *The Devil's Disciple*, Act III, p. 249.

The epigrammatic nub is in the 'British War Office', and the condensation arises, as so often in epigram and paradox, from the word
play, 'stand up' being used in both a physical and a moral sense.

THE DEVIL. . . . An Englishman thinks he is moral when he is only
uncomfortable.

> *Man and Superman*, Act III, p. 374.

PATIOMKIN. . . . Woman reduces us all to the common denominator.

> *Great Catherine*, Sc. I, p. 806.

In such epigrammatic astringency, almost free from verbal legerder-
main, Shaw's wit enters the domain of poetry—the poetry of the intellect.[9] For wit as well as poetry is 'the instrument of a greater and
more rapid concentration.'[10] Through condensation it achieves an
allusiveness, richness of association, an intellectual insight which spurns
pettifogging modifications. Through what is left unsaid and the condensation of what is said, Shaw's prose ensures the necessary indirection
for the reader's participation, which his rather too direct satirical vehemence might otherwise forfeit.

But it would be a misunderstanding of the nature of poetic condensation if we looked for this 'concentration' only in the more palpable
witticisms. Poetry does not necessarily say more in fewer words than
prose. Its concentration consists in the communication of a more vivid
impression of what it does say through concrete and sensuous language and through concrete and sensuous imagery. Wit, as the poetry
of the intellect and not of the senses, eschews the sensuous but retains
the concrete. Paradox and epigram are abstractions almost by definition, and their condensation is achieved through the abstraction of
universality and not through the concreteness of the particular; but,
although untrue of witticisms, Bergson's comment that 'Several

---

[9] Bergson, p. 106, 'In short, he [the poet] would turn into a wit by simply re-
solving to be no longer a poet in feeling, but only in intelligence.'
[10] J. Middleton Murry, *The Problem of Style*, 1922, p. 123.

authors, Jean Paul amongst them, have noticed that humour delights
in concrete terms, technical details, definite facts'[11] is substantially true
of witty writing in general, and 'concrete terms' and 'definite facts',
while making greater impact, certainly do not make for brevity. Even
such a highly compressed image as Shakespeare's

Now does he feel
His secret murders sticking on his hands;[12]

incomparably superior as it is in overtones and associations to an abstract paraphrase: 'The victim dies, but guilt survives', is not so brief.
Shaw's witty writing, as distinct from his witticisms, is, like Shake-
spearean metaphor, dramatically effective by the concrete profusion
which imparts shape and substance to the evanescent spoken word.

Extracts from a discussion play, *Getting Married*, illustrate this omni-
present proclivity of Shavian wit:

> THE BISHOP. If we are going to discuss ethical questions we must
> begin by giving the devil fair play. Boxer never does. England never
> does. We always assume that the devil is guilty: and we wont allow
> him to prove his innocence, because it would be against public
> morals if he succeeded. We used to do the same with prisoners
> accused of high treason. And the consequence is that we overreach
> ourselves; and the devil gets the better of us after all. Perhaps thats
> what most of us intend him to do.
>
> *Getting Married*, p. 556.

Such is the form in which ethical questions are discussed. A philosopher's disquisition on the unsoundness of an irrational morality
would obviously be less witty and less dramatic than the appearance of
conventional sin incarnate in the person of the devil.

> LESBIA. Yes: I must have my own separate house, or my own
> separate part of a house. Boxer smokes: I cant endure tobacco.
> Boxer believes that an open window means death from cold and
> exposure to the night air: I must have fresh air always. We can be

[11] Bergson, pp. 127–8.
[12] Shakespeare, *Macbeth*, ed. J. D. Wilson, Cambridge, 1947, Act V, Sc. II, ll.
16–17, p. 74.

friends; but we cant live together; and that must be put in the agreement.

Ibid., p. 571.

Even for the unmarried Lesbia the problems of marriage take on a married form.

SOAMES. Does that help?

HOTCHKISS. No.

SOAMES. Then pray for light.

HOTCHKISS. No: I am a snob, not a beggar. (*He sits down in the General's chair.*)

COLLINS. We dont seem to be getting on, do we? Miss Edith: you and Mr. Sykes had better go off to church and settle the right and wrong of it afterwards. Itll ease your minds, believe me: I speak from experience. You will burn your boats, as one might say.

SOAMES. We should never burn our boats. It is death in life.

COLLINS. Well, Father, I will say for you that you have views of your own and are not afraid to out with them. But some of us are of a more cheerful disposition. On the Borough Council now, you would be in a minority of one. You must take human nature as it is.

SOAMES. Upon what compulsion must I? I'll take divine nature as it is. I'll not hold a candle to the devil.

THE BISHOP. Thats a very unchristian way of treating the devil.

Ibid., pp. 573-4.

Shaw makes the three metaphors 'pray for light', 'burn your boats', and 'hold a candle to the devil' even more corporeal by extension or repetition. In the first and third metaphors a coadjutant and more subtle connection between concrete terms and witty writing can be seen; for the extensions exploit—not very successfully in the first, as the satirical comment on prayer is obscure—the humour of infusing a literal flavour into the figurative.

This amplification through the concrete, if used to the same extent in purely polemical writing, would become intolerably tedious. But just as dramatic dialogue needs strength of assertion to be effective, so does dramatic wit, because of the more fugitive medium and the necessity for immediate response, need to be underlined more than ordinary written wit. Sometimes the amplification almost takes the form of explanation:

> THE CHAPLAIN. Englishmen heretics!!! (*Appealing to Warwick*) My lord: must we endure this? His lordship is beside himself. How can what an Englishman believes be heresy? It is a contradiction in terms.
>
> *Saint Joan*, Sc. IV., p. 983.

The Chaplain's unconscious witticism 'How can what an Englishman believes be heresy' is underlined both before and after. In written wit, 'It is a contradiction in terms' would be inexcusable, but in spoken wit it provides a period of gestation. That the thickheaded chaplain is responsible for the underlining is an irrelevant consideration, for the more thickheaded the speaker the less likely would he think it necessary to elucidate such an obvious libel.

> THE BISHOP. . . . He longed to take holy orders, but didnt dare to, because his father had a weak heart and habitually threatened to drop dead if anybody hurt his feelings. You may have noticed that people with weak hearts are the tyrants of English family life.
>
> *Getting Married*, p. 569.

Even in spoken wit the underlining here seems less excusable. But the witty remark 'and habitually threatened to drop dead if anybody hurt his feelings' occurs in the middle of a speech, and the Bishop has to be provided with words which add nothing new so that he can talk his way through the laugh. The forecasting of the response of even a specified audience to a comedy line cannot be undertaken with any confidence, and Shaw usually played safe—sometimes too safe.

It can be observed that this underlining is the work of the loose extension. Structural periodicity is unfriendly to wit, particularly dramatic wit, which should be loose so that it can be acted with pauses of varying length to give the speaker time for a gesture, a significant inflection, a change of tone, and a change of breath. Even a spoken epigram requires a pause and a slight change of tone to mark the omission of the trend of thought. And even the periodic effect imparted by rhythm is more favourable to declamation than acting, and is, as has already been noted, usually reserved by Shaw for polemical wit which hopes to convert to a positive attitude, or for the necessary periodic prelude to the loose addition of an anticlimax.

But although far less characteristic of dramatic wit and seldom used by Shaw, the structurally periodic sentence has some small place; and can provide both the climactic approach and the anticlimactic shock:

> APOLLODORUS. Majesty: when a stupid man is doing something he is ashamed of, he always declares that it is his duty.
>
> *Caesar and Cleopatra*, Act III, p. 275.

If the main clause were put first: 'A stupid man always declares that it is his duty when he is doing something that he is ashamed of', there is the awkwardness of a prepositional ending and a failure to appreciate that it is the claims of duty which are being derided and which should therefore be left to the end to form the nub of the witticism. Furthermore, as deliberative modification, heightened in this case by the necessary inclusion of the 'stupid', is hostile to wit, particularly epigrammatic wit, which, ideally, should be universal in its application, it is better to have done with it as early as possible in the sentence. Priority of 'if' and 'when' modifications is common enough in witticism:

> DON JUAN. . . . When the military man approaches, the world locks up its spoons and packs off its womankind.
>
> *Man and Superman*, Act III, p. 379.

The universality of the epigram this time undergoes a vocational modification. Incidentally, the inclusion of 'packs off' affords a further interesting example of the preservation of polemical rhythm even at the expense of the humour of a condensed sentence ('locks up its spoons and its womankind').

> AUBREY. . . . But there was an extraordinary sympathy between our lower centres; and when after ten days she threw me over for another man I was restrained from murder and suicide only by the most resolute exercise of my reasoning powers, my determination to be a civilized man, and fear of the police.
>
> *Too True to be Good*, Act II, p. 1147.

The sentence is periodic in form in so far as the subordinate clause 'when after ten days she threw me over for another man' precedes the main clause, but the main clause is loose in structure. If it remained periodic throughout and continued 'it was only by the most resolute exercise of my reasoning powers, my determination to be a civilized man, and my fear of the police that I was restrained from murder and suicide', unwanted and inappropriate dignity would be gained and the anticlimactic humour of 'fear of the police', which gains in brevity and humorous universality by the omission of the 'my', would be lost. Thus does a sentence which is, so to speak, periodic in conception wander off into less majestic channels so that it may the more easily run to wit.

M'COMAS. . . . When a man makes an unsuitable marriage (nobody's fault, you know, but purely accidental incompatibility of tastes); when he is deprived by that misfortune of the domestic sympathy which, I take it, is what a man marries for; when, in short, his wife is rather worse than no wife at all (through no fault of her own, of course), is it to be wondered at if he makes matters worse at first by blaming her, and even, in his desperation, by occasionally drinking himself into a violent condition or seeking sympathy elsewhere?

You Never Can Tell, Act III, pp. 205-6.

Structurally this is a very long periodic sentence which cannot be ended before 'violent condition'. But although its main purpose is not comedic, it gains in humour and acting potential, and loses in undue solemnity by means of a series of loose parenthetical interpolations.

WAITER. . . . But as I say to him, wheres the difference after all? If I must put on a dress coat to shew what I am, sir, he must put on a wig and gown to shew what he is. If my income is mostly tips, and theres a pretence that I dont get them, why, his income is mostly fees, sir; and I understand theres a pretence that he dont get them! If he likes society, and his profession brings him into contact with all ranks, so does mine too, sir. If it's a little against a barrister to have a waiter for his father, sir, it's a little against a waiter to have a barrister for a son: many people consider it a great liberty, sir, I assure you, sir. Can I get you anything else, sir?

Ibid., Act II, p. 194.

Each sentence could be said to be structurally periodic, but the initial clauses are only superficially conditional. With a few changes in punctuation, the 'ifs' could be omitted and the ensuing looseness of form would lay bare the device of antithesis, which is often witty in itself and, like most other figures, almost invariably gains in wit if used cumulatively. It is perhaps in such antithesis that the witticism, although not at its funniest, is in its most anticlimactic and satirical form, with the closest of juxtapositions for 'two ideas fundamentally inharmonious'. And the closer the juxtaposition the looser the structure.

Periodic structure, then, plays but little part in the dissonance or the surprise of wit. Looseness of form is also favourable to poetic concentration; and in this context the consideration of poetic concentration bridges the somewhat artificial gap between sound and sense, just as poetry bridges the gap between the primal art of music and the cerebrations of expository prose. And style implies the introduction of musical and poetic qualities into 'plain prose'. The poetic quality of Shaw's wit shapes and tempers his prose into a remarkable and delightful instrument for sociological drama.

PART II

Sense

CHAPTER I

Inversion

I. BASIC PARADOX

THAT many rhetorical devices, such as alliteration, assonance, epizeuxis, and condensation, are of equal service to both tragedian and satirist is sufficient reminder of the primacy of sense over sound. But the primacy of sense, although perhaps self-evident, is not self-sufficient; and if there is a real interdependence between sense and sound, the analytical distinction between inevitability and surprise in the realm of sound may possibly be valid in the realm of sense.

It will be more convenient if surprise is treated first, for the transition from the juxtaposition of two sounds fundamentally inharmonious to the juxtaposition of 'two ideas fundamentally inharmonious'[1] is easily made. And it is clear that in making such a transition we are entering into a field which extends from the surprise of the anti-climactic inversion of the expected—inherent in the thought-play and word-play of the epigram and paradox—to the limits of the comic cosmos. Aristotle's standpoint (as presented by Hobbes), 'Also paradoxes are graceful, so men inwardly do believe them; for they have in them somewhat like to those jests that are grounded upon the similitude of words, which have usually one sense, and in the present another; and somewhat like to those jests which are grounded upon the deceiving of a man's expectation'[2] is probably the original idea from which the modern theories of wit as 'deceived expectation' are derived. Kant's 'strained expectation being suddenly reduced to nothing',[3] Bergson's jack-in-the-box[4] as a basic comic conception, and Max Eastman's

---

[1] Nicoll, p. 48 (quoted p. 29).
[2] Aristotle's *Rhetoric*, A Digest by Thomas Hobbes, Bk. III, Chap. X, Everyman's Ed., 1949, p. 159.
[3] *Critique of Aesthetic Judgment*, tr. by James Creed Meredith, 1911, p. 199.
[4] Bergson, pp. 69–77.

definition of laughter as a compensation for disappointment[5] are, for instance, all dependent on the idea of deceived expectation. Ignoring, as it does, the element of inevitability, this idea may be inadequate as a complete theory of laughter; but from a structural point of view it provides us with a key to much of the wit and satire of Bernard Shaw, with the inversion of the familiar into the unfamiliar and the unfamiliar into the familiar. Deceived expectation is also the basis of epigram and paradox; the basis of many of the situations, arguments, and characterisations within the plays; and it is the key to the themes of some of the greatest of the plays, which are in effect expanded paradoxes.

The paradox as witticism is usually expressed in a verbal form which is contradictory or whimsical; but any proposition which is an inversion of generally received opinion can be defined as paradox, and if we accept such a definition, the paradoxical nature of the themes of most of Shaw's plays becomes apparent. In the witticism, condensation entails, as already shown, the omission of the intervening trend of thought which would otherwise constitute some kind of proof of the proposition, but in the paradox expanded into a theme the proof will not only be present but will be the main concern of the play; for Shaw is concerned not with what he calls the 'inanities of action' but with ideas, with demonstrating that his paradoxes are unexpected truths and not perversions of the truth. The paradoxical form in which he presents his ideas is, of course, one of the means by which he transforms an exercise in pamphleteering into an art-form. Satire is usually the criticism of the accepted, and, if unadorned invective is excluded, artistic indirection is implicit in all satirical wit from the simplest sarcasm to the subtlest forms of irony. And the construction of a satirical play should be such as to provide the most effective means of converting the indirect into the direct, of demonstrating that the basic paradox is only seemingly untrue.

In his reaction from the 'well-made' play, Shaw thought, or pretended to think, that his plays had no construction. Nevertheless, plays which involve the proving of a thesis and not the unfolding of a plot often assume a pattern similar to that of the Socratic Method, which also has the proof of a view contrary to received opinion as its aim. There is a first stage, in which there is a general acceptance by most of the characters of the everyday or unparadoxical standpoint. This may or may not be accompanied by the celebrated Socratic Irony, in which

[5] Max Eastman, *Enjoyment of Laughter*, New York, 1936.

the representative of the paradoxical view simulates ignorance and a touching desire to learn. The second and longest stage, the Definition, consists of a gradual and empirical revelation of the worthlessness of the accepted and the soundness of the paradoxical view. The third stage, the Maieutic, sets forth the implications of the new standpoint. The three stages in Shaw's plays are perhaps more mutually interpenetrative than the exposition, complication and dénouement of the drama of action or the three corresponding stages in the Socratic Dialogue. A Shavian play cannot be reduced to a formula.[6] Nevertheless, for a great number of the plays such a frame of reference is apparent. *Major Barbara*, with its highly paradoxical theme that money is the root of all virtue and that poverty is 'the worst of all crimes',[7] provides a useful testing ground.

The first, or Irony stage, consists of a statement of the orthodox point of view as represented by Lady Britomart, whose objection to her husband is that he does not keep up the appearances required by conventional morality; by her son Stephen, a naïve moral absolutist whose objection to his father is that he is a social pariah for making millions out of selling cannons; by Barbara who represents the Christian standpoint that poverty is no bar to the purity of heart necessary to salvation; and by Cusins, a Greek scholar, who represents the humanism of Oxford and West Ham.

Even in this Irony stage the beginnings of the Definition stage can be seen; Stephen is a pretentious prig and Lady Britomart a hypocrite, though amiable and almost self-acknowledged. Barbara and Cusins, however, are presented in a favourable light; for the conversion to the paradoxical point of view, to be effective, must be an intellectual *tour de force* and not merely the overcoming of silly prejudices. For this reason, too, Shaw sweeps aside the usual plea that 'the more destructive war becomes, the sooner it will be abolished'.[8] Such a spuriously moral defence would make the fundamental paradox less forceful.

Undershaft, the arms manufacturer, is the protagonist of the paradoxical point of view, and the exponent of what Lady Britomart calls a 'religion of wrongness'.[9] He has 'an engaging simplicity of character',[10] is quite submissive to his wife, and is diffident and deferential in

---

[6] See, for example, the varied interpretations of *Candida* as set out in Arthur H. Nethercot, *Men and Supermen*, Cambridge (Massachusetts), 1954, pp. 7–17.
[7] *Major Barbara*, Act III, p. 498.   [8] *Ibid.*, Act I, p. 468.
[9] *Ibid.*, Act I, p. 463.   [10] *Ibid.*, Act I, p. 466.

manner to everybody. 'Never mind me, my dear. As you know, I am not a gentleman; and I was never educated.'[11] He has the *ingénu* attitude of Socrates which we have already noticed in Lady Cicely in *Captain Brassbound's Conversion*, and, by the end of the first act he has on a purely personal plane won over the younger generation to such an extent that Lady Britomart even talks about fathers who come along and steal the children's affections from the mother.[12]

The second, or Definition stage, is divided into two parts. Act II, set in the yard of a Salvation Army shelter, ends in the debacle of the Christian position, with Barbara saying 'My God: why hast thou forsaken me?'[13] and 'Peter: I'm like you now. Cleaned out, and lost my job.'[14] Act III, set partly in Lady Britomart's residence and partly in Undershaft's arms foundry, sees first the dialectical rout of Stephen and then a practical vindication of Undershaft's views in the form of the model community dependent on the manufacture of arms. It must be borne in mind that only a structural comparison with Socratic Method is being made. Detachment and an exhaustive elimination mark the Definition stage in Socrates, whereas Shaw, both by temperament and dramatic necessity, immediately whisks his audiences off to grounds of his own choosing.

The Maieutic stage sees the conversion of Cusins and Barbara to the paradoxical view, propounded anew by Cusins: 'Then the way of life lies through the factory of death?'[15] And so that once again nothing may lessen the force of the paradox, the conversion comes after Undershaft has told them of the good news from Manchuria about a new aerial battleship which has wiped out a fort with three hundred soldiers in it. 'To be wealthy,' says Undershaft, 'is with me a point of honor for which I am prepared to kill at the risk of my own life. This preparedness, is, as he says, the final test of sincerity.'[16] The implication of the Definition stage in *Major Barbara* is that we can only work to a higher end through reality, through institutions as they are, through human beings who are as yet imperfectly developed, and that it is useless to build Utopias on absolutist sands. For paradox, as a form of wit, is rational in conception and intention and exposes the sham and immorality which often lie concealed behind received opinion and taboo morality.

---

11 *Ibid.*, Act I, p. 467.   12 *Ibid.*, Act I, p. 470.
13 *Ibid.*, Act II, p. 485.   14 *Ibid.*, Act II, p. 486.
15 *Ibid.*, Act III, p. 503.   16 *Major Barbara*, Prefaces, p. 120.

The paradox of *John Bull's Other Island*, emphasised by a paradoxical treatment of the English and Irish national characters and Anglo-Irish relations, depends on the same pragmatic and relativist standpoint. 'The fact is,' says Broadbent, the English entrepreneur who wants to bring the blessings of capitalist development to Ireland, 'there are only two qualities in the world: efficiency and inefficiency, and only two sorts of people: the efficient and the inefficient.'[17] That the irony of the first stage is inverted in this play, that Broadbent is not a simulated but a genuine *ingénu*, is not significant structurally. Again the Definition stage exposes a reality of squalor, gullibility, brutishness, and superstition behind the romantic façade of 'auld Ireland'. In the Maieutic stage at the end, Keegan, representing a one and indivisible morality, is not converted in quite the same way as Major Barbara. 'For four wicked centuries the world has dreamed this foolish dream of efficiency; and the end is not yet. But the end will come.'[18] But because the end is not yet, he is acquiescent. He says that he may even vote for Broadbent in the parliamentary elections.[19] 'Mr Broadbent spends his life inefficiently admiring the thoughts of great men, and efficiently serving the cupidity of base money hunters. We spend our lives efficiently sneering at him and doing nothing. Which of us has any right to reproach the other?'[20] The paradox, even if it is not universally valid, is valid for the time and place.

A dozen other plays follow a similar, although sometimes a looser, pattern. In *Arms and the Man*, the conventional attitudes towards military heroism and the 'higher love' are presented in the Irony stage, debunked in the Definition stage, and rejected by their erstwhile protagonists in the Maieutic stage. In *Man and Superman*, the main theme is a paradoxical view of courtship with woman as the hunter. If the theme is for us less paradoxical, and therefore less amusing, Shaw is in no small part responsible. The paradox has become a widely accepted truth. In the inverted melodrama of *The Devil's Disciple*, the devil turns out to be an angel. In *Candida*, the stronger of the two men turns out to be the weaker, and the strong husband turns out to be a domestic pet. In *The Apple Cart*, the weaker turns out to be the stronger, a constitutional monarch, by exploiting the resources of democracy, triumphing over a democratically constituted cabinet. In *How He Lied to Her Hus-*

---

[17] *John Bull's Other Island*, Act IV, p. 449.
[18] *Ibid.*, Act IV, p. 450.
[19] *Ibid.*, Act IV, p. 449.
[20] *Ibid.*, Act IV, p. 451.

band, the husband is angry because another man is not in love with his wife. In *Widowers' Houses* and *Mrs Warren's Profession*, the innocent are as guilty or more guilty than the guilty, the emphasis being on collective responsibility for individual sin.

Always in Shaw there is an urge to include or underline a basic paradox even if the play cannot be constructed around it. In the much criticised epilogue of *St Joan*, artistic indirection is abandoned in Shaw's desire to demonstrate that the basic paradox, the rejection of a saint, has an application far beyond the exigencies of the medieval situation. After centuries of lip-service she is still rejected; and it is significant to the present analysis that, although it is an epilogue to a tragedy, it is comic in conception and farcical in consummation. The paradox could not be brought out in the tragic inevitability of Joan's end; for in tragedy, paradox is woven into the very stuff of life and must be expected and accepted, whereas in comedy, paradox provides an alternative to the generally accepted.

In *The Doctor's Dilemma*, also described by Shaw as a tragedy, the paradox of a woman being in love with a scoundrel is underlined in an otherwise inconsequential fifth act, which once again converts a personal and emotional issue into an intellectual and universal issue by divorcing it from the death of Dubedat. In *Pygmalion*, Shaw adds a postscript in undramatic form to eliminate romantic assumptions, and to point out that the apparently remarkable transfiguration of Eliza Doolittle is 'common enough'.[21] In a similar postscript to *Androcles and the Lion*, he explains that the apparently unique phenomena of early Christianity and its persecution by Rome is the customary pattern of social and political behaviour.[22] The paradox of *Pygmalion* is that apparently deep-rooted class differences are founded on mere externals, and the paradox of *Androcles and the Lion* is that the judges are often more wicked than the judged. Both plays suffer from not having the truth of these paradoxes demonstrated clearly enough in the plays themselves. *Androcles and the Lion* degenerates into farce, and recently there has been little difficulty in degrading *Pygmalion* into musical comedy. Dramatic shortcomings cannot be saved by postscripts, and the necessity of postscripts for Shaw is evidence of these shortcomings, and evidence that the basic paradox is the axis on which the greater Shavian comedy turns.

[21] *Pygmalion*, Postscript, p. 751.
[22] *Androcles and the Lion*, Postscript, pp. 702-3.

2. TRANSPOSITION OF KEY

The basic paradox, a turning of the ideological tables, is then an integral part of Shavian comedy. But by itself it is not an indisputable criterion of comedy. Most of the sociological drama of the late nineteenth and early twentieth centuries developed theses which were contrary to received opinion, but little of it was comedy. The sociological drama of Ibsen, Granville Barker, Galsworthy, and Brieux is cast in a tragic mould; for the inversion implicit in paradox is not reflected in the inversion in tone which Bergson calls 'transposing the natural expression of an idea into another key'.[23] Shaw continually converts the great into the small, the romantic into the prosaic, the solemn into the frivolous, the superhuman into the human, the remote into the familiar, or—to generalise the transposition into the comic formula—the expected into the unexpected. In *The Apple Cart*, a constitutional crisis is treated on the level of a family argument. In *Heartbreak House*, the crisis of Western civilisation is treated on the level of a comedy of manners. In *Man and Superman*, the promptings of the Life Force are reduced to the level of a male spider's courtship. In *Caesar and Cleopatra*, the destinies of a nation are treated on the level of a palace intrigue. The change of tone is not, of course, unrelieved but it is usually dominant. It is what has been called earlier 'ordinary understatement',[24] which is anticlimactic in relation to the general situation. It serves not only to rid the theme of romantic associations and accretions but also to rid the presentation of the theme of the too obvious didacticism which is to be found in *Widowers' Houses* and *Mrs Warren's Profession*, two plays which were written before Shaw's comedic talent was fully developed, and against both, particularly *Widowers' Houses*, the charge of pamphleteering has often been brought.

This transposition of key, eliminating, as it does, an emotional in favour of an intellectual and witty approach, is responsible for the famous and infamous Shaw heartlessness. An example of murder treated as a minor misdemeanour by this technique has already been given.[25] Here the subject is a mere execution:

BURGOYNE (*sympathetically*). Now there, Mr Anderson, you talk like a civilian, if you will excuse my saying so. Have you any idea of the average marksmanship of the army of His Majesty King

---

[23] Bergson, p. 123.   [24] See pp. 27–8.   [25] See pp. 20–1.

George the Third? If we make you up a firing party, what will happen? Half of them will miss you: the rest will make a mess of the business and leave you to the provo-marshal's pistol. Whereas we can hang you in a perfectly workmanlike and agreeable way. (*Kindly*) Let me persuade you to be hanged, Mr Anderson?

JUDITH (*sick with horror*). My God!

The Devil's Disciple, Act III, p. 243.

Judith's emotional attitude seems to make her unconscious of the superiority of 'Let me persuade you to be hanged' to 'Let me persuade you that hanging would be easier for you'.

BURGOYNE. Mr Anderson——

SWINDON. His name is Dudgeon, sir, Richard Dudgeon. He is an impostor.

BURGOYNE (*brusquely*). Nonsense, sir: you hanged Dudgeon at Springtown.

RICHARD. It was my uncle, General.

BURGOYNE. Oh, your uncle. (*To Swindon, handsomely*) I beg your pardon, Major Swindon. (*Swindon acknowledges the apology stiffly. Burgoyne turns to Richard.*) We are somewhat unfortunate in our relations with your family. Well, Mr Dudgeon, what I wanted to ask you is this. Who is (*reading the name from the letter*) William Maindeck Parshotter?

RICHARD. He is the Mayor of Springtown.

BURGOYNE. Is William—Maindeck and so on—a man of his word?

RICHARD. Is he selling you anything?

BURGOYNE. No.

RICHARD. Then you may depend on him.

BURGOYNE. Thank you, Mr—'m Dudgeon. By the way, since you are not Mr Anderson, do we still—eh, Major Swindon? (*meaning 'do we still hang him?'*)

RICHARD. The arrangements are unaltered, General.

BURGOYNE. Ah, indeed. I am sorry. Good morning, Mr Dudgeon. Good morning, madam.

Ibid., Act III, p. 245.

Richard, by returning civility for civility, contributes handsomely to the general atmosphere of detachment, delicacy, and to the diffidence of the understatement which scarcely states at all. He, too, although less urbane than Burgoyne, is a realist, and therefore, in Shaw's book, a man of wit. That later, just before the moment of the execution, he rounds on Burgoyne with 'And if you think I'm obliged to you for hanging me in a gentlemanly way, youre wrong there too. I take the whole business in devilish bad part. . . .'[26] shows no inconsistency of character. Indeed, 'devilish bad part', masquerading as a strong expression of feeling, is a masterly understatement.

> ANDERSON (*exhaling a deep breath of relief, and dabbing his perspiring brow with his handkerchief*). Thank God, I was in time!
> BURGOYNE (*calm as ever, and still watch in hand.*) Ample time, sir. Plenty of time. I should never dream of hanging any gentleman by an American clock. (*He puts up his watch.*)

· · · · · ·

> BURGOYNE (*to Swindon*). You look disappointed, Major Swindon.
> SWINDON. You look defeated, General Burgoyne.
> BURGOYNE. I am, sir; and I am humane enough to be glad of it.
>
> *Ibid.*, Act III, p. 249.

For Burgoyne, the seemingly callous man of wit, is, in strong contrast to his foil, the righteously unpleasant Major Swindon, an essentially humane man. It is by such contrasts, indeed, that Shaw, who is usually interested in converting others to his opinions, gains the sympathy of his audiences who are intellectually diverse but emotionally similar. Contrary to the generally accepted view and contrary to his own view, Shaw does not eschew emotion. By making his unwitty characters ridiculous or reprehensible, their opponents are thrown up into favourable relief. In *The Devil's Disciple*, we not only favour Burgoyne over against Swindon; but from the outset, because of the impossible Mrs Dudgeon and because of his kindness to Essie, we are on Richard's side. The heart of gold lurking behind a caustic exterior is a stock character of fiction, which Shaw exploits with a protean and sophisticated skill. The wit in itself also enlists our sympathies on the side of the witty characters, for there is a strong tendency to side with

26 *The Devil's Disciple*, Act III, p. 248.

the winner of a verbal duel. Laughter, too, provides a release from the restrictions and repressions of the socially conditioned emotions. 'It is the liberation of the natural man from the ties and conventions of society.'[27] Shaw's famous 'Not bloody likely'[28] is merely an extreme, although because of its context not a crude example of release from taboo.

3. INVERSION OF CHARACTER

One of the chief means of achieving a transposition of key is, the presentation of characters in an unexpected light, by inverting the customary correlation between character and calling, between attitude and status. King Magnus stands in strong contrast to the dehumanised figurehead of popular fancy, for *The Apple Cart* could not have been written around a conventional king who concealed the essential weakness of a constitutional monarch under the externals of regal dignity and restraint. Wit is itself a most unkingly attribute:

> MAGNUS. It was perhaps indelicate. But you all allude so freely to your own powers—to the supremacy of Parliament and the voice of the people and so forth—that I fear I have lost any little delicacy I ever possessed. If you may flourish your thunderbolts why may I not shoulder my little popgun of a veto and strut up and down with it for a moment?
>
> *The Apple Cart*, Act I, p. 1018.

Major Barbara could not have been written around the armament manufacturer of sinister and pacifist renown, who justifies his activities with specious arguments and stills his conscience with good works instead of good workshops. Once again wit is not usually associated with a dealer in death:

> UNDERSHAFT. Not at all. The more destructive war becomes the more fascinating we find it. No, Mr Lomax: I am obliged to you for making the usual excuse for my trade; but I am not ashamed of it. I am not one of those men who keep their morals and their business in water-tight compartments. All the spare money my trade rivals spend on hospitals, cathedrals, and other receptacles for conscience

---

[27] Nicoll, p. 155.   [28] *Pygmalion*, Act III, p. 736.

money, I devote to experiments and researches in improved methods of destroying life and property. I have always done so; and I always shall. Therefore your Christmas card moralities of peace on earth and goodwill among men are of no use to me. Your Christianity, which enjoins you to resist not evil, and to turn the other cheek, would make me a bankrupt. My morality—my religion—must have a place for cannons and torpedoes in it.

Major Barbara, Act I, p. 468.

Caesar and Cleopatra, too, could not have been written around a conqueror cut on the conventional lines of Marlowe's Tamburlaine or even Shakespeare's Henry V. Indeed, Shaw, conscious of an inconsistency between the Caesar of his play and the Caesar of history, has to put a speech into his mouth regretting his past:

CAESAR. No, by the gods! would that it had been! Vengeance at least is human. No, I say: those severed right hands, and the brave Vercingetorix basely strangled in a vault beneath the Capitol, were (*with shuddering satire*) a wise severity, a necessary protection to the commonwealth, a duty of statesmanship—follies and fictions ten times bloodier than honest vengeance! What a fool was I then! To think that men's lives should be at the mercy of such fools!

Caesar and Cleopatra, Act II, p. 267.

Bentley points out that Shaw's Caesar, Napoleon and Joan are not debunkings, they are variants 'of the popular legend: the granite-faced Caesar, Napoleon as he appears in David's portraits, Joan as interpreted by Schiller or Mark Twain'.[29] Stereotyping and dehumanisation always increase with distance, and the further we are in time, place, or way of life, the easier it is to introduce variants from the legend, which often depend on little more than the addition of a few human characteristics. The average theatre-goer does not number kings, conquerors, and armament manufacturers amongst his friends. King Magnus is probably a less humorous character to a king, while Shaw's Caesar would probably not have been funny to Napoleon or Stalin. The plays abound in men and women who are eminent or remote in rank, reputation, or position:

[29] Bentley, *Shaw*, p. 181.

THE BISHOP. Yes, you! think of what it would do for you. For her sake you would come to care unselfishly and diligently for money instead of being selfishly and lazily indifferent to it. For her sake you would come to care in the same way for preferment. For her sake you would come to care for your health, your appearance, the good opinion of your fellow creatures, and all the really important things that make men work and strive instead of mooning and nursing their salvation.

Getting Married, p. 582.

Worldliness becomes wittier when propounded by a bishop. And lachrymose love becomes more ludicrous when its victim is a general 'resplendent in full-dress uniform, with many medals and orders':[30]

THE GENERAL. Tricks! Ha! Well, I'll try to break myself of it; but I think she might bear with me in a little thing like that. She knows that her name sticks in my throat. Better call her your sister than try to call her L—(*he almost breaks down*) L—well, call her by her name and make a fool of myself by crying. (*He sits down at the near end of the table.*)

Ibid., p. 547.

But almost equally remote to the average theatre-goer, although less remote today, is the other end of the social ladder. To an audience which associates the lower orders with loose morals the prudery of Eliza is more amusing. She is even reluctant to name the offensive object:

HIGGINS. I'm glad the bathroom met with your approval.
LIZA. It didn't: not all of it; and I dont care who hears me say it. Mrs Pearce knows.
HIGGINS. What was wrong, Mrs Pearce?
MRS PEARCE (*blandly*) Oh, nothing, sir. It doesnt matter.
LIZA. I had a good mind to break it. I didnt know which way to look. But I hung a towel over it, I did.
HIGGINS. Over what?
MRS PEARCE. Over the looking-glass, sir.

[30] *Getting Married*, p. 547.

HIGGINS. Doolittle: you have brought your daughter up too strictly.

DOOLITTLE. Me! I never brought her up at all, except to give her a lick of a strap now and again. Dont put it on me, Governor. She aint accustomed to it, you see: thats all. But she'll soon pick up your free-and-easy ways.

Pygmalion, Act II, p. 731.

To a middle-class audience of the nineties the class inversion contained in the following dialogue must also have been highly diverting. The waiter's unconcern provides a typically Shavian comic inversion within an inversion:

DOLLY. Is your son a waiter too, William?

WAITER (*serving Gloria with fowl*). Oh no, miss: he's too impetuous. He's at the Bar.

M'COMAS (*patronizingly*). A potman, eh?

WAITER (*with a touch of melancholy, as if recalling a disappointment softened by time*). No, sir: the other bar. Your profession, sir. A Q.C., sir.

M'COMAS (*embarrassed*). I'm sure I beg your pardon.

WAITER. Not at all, sir. Very natural mistake, I'm sure, sir. Ive often wished he was a potman, sir. Would have been off my hands ever so much sooner, sir. (*Aside to Valentine, who is again in difficulties*) Salt at your elbow, sir. (*Resuming*) Yes, sir: had to support him until he was thirty-seven, sir. But doing well now, sir: very satisfactory indeed, sir. Nothing less than fifty guineas, sir.

M'COMAS. Democracy, Crampton! Modern democracy!

WAITER (*calmly*). No, sir, not democracy: only education, sir, Scholarships, sir. Cambridge Local, sir. Sidney Sussex College, sir. (*Dolly plucks his sleeve and whispers as he bends down.*) Stone ginger, miss? Right, miss. (*To M'Comas*) Very good thing for him, sir: he never had any turn for real work, sir. (*He goes into the hotel, leaving the company somewhat overwhelmed by his son's eminence.*)

You Never Can Tell, Act II, p. 191.

In the following dialogues an inversion similar to that which sustains Barrie's *Admirable Crichton* is exploited:

TANNER. You think it's simply bad taste in me to chaff him, Tavy. But youre wrong. This man takes more trouble to drop his aitches than ever his father did to pick them up. It's a mark of caste to him. I have never met anybody more swollen with the pride of class than Enry is.

STRAKER. Easy, easy! A little moderation, Mr Tanner.

TANNER. A little moderation, Tavy, you observe. You would tell me to draw it mild. But this chap has been educated. Whats more, he knows that we havnt. What was that Board School of yours, Straker?

STRAKER. Sherbrooke Road.

TANNER. Sherbrooke Road! Would any of us say Rugby! Harrow! Eton! in that tone of intellectual snobbery? Sherbrooke Road is a place where boys learn something: Eton is a boy farm where we are sent because we are nuisances at home, and because in after life, whenever a Duke is mentioned, we can claim him as an old school-fellow.

Man and Superman, Act II, p. 352.

TANNER (*impressively*). I trust, Enry, that, as between employer and engineer, I shall always know how to keep my proper distance, and not intrude my private affairs on you. Even our business arrangements are subject to the approval of your Trade Union. But dont abuse your advantages. Let me remind you that Voltaire said that what was too silly to be said could be sung.

STRAKER. It wasnt Voltaire: it was Bow Mar Shay.

TANNER. I stand corrected: Beaumarchais of course.

Ibid., Act II, p. 360.

But, as an opponent of sentimental socialism, Shaw does not practise the inversion of levelling up so often as he does that of levelling down. He is concerned with abolishing rather than eulogizing the working class, and the lower orders in *Major Barbara* and *John Bull's Other Island* are inversions of the delusions of romantic revolutionaries. But the inversion is too esoteric to be more than grimly humorous even to the initiated, and Snobby Price of *Major Barbara* and Patsy Farrel of *John Bull's Other Island* are wry representatives rather than comic characters. It is only when the satire on revolutionaries is more direct and more appropriate to the theatre, as it is with Mendoza's motley bunch of brigands in *Man and Superman*, that the humour leavens the sociological purpose.

4. INVERSION OF THE SEXES

But perhaps for comedy the most fundamental of all Shaw's character inversions is epitomised in the words of Charteris in *The Philanderer*: 'No. Unhand me, Julia. (*He tries to get away: she holds him.*) If you dont let me go, I'll scream for help.'[31] It is an inversion which depends for its unexpectedness on the repudiation of the orthodox relation of the sexes as portrayed in melodrama, which, perhaps more than tragedy, is the literary antithesis of comedy and embodies most completely popular romantic conventions. Comedy, as Meredith pointed out,[32] can only exist where women have a high status and it turns largely on the battle of the sexes. 'Now we may have whole series of tragedies,' says Allardyce Nicoll, 'which depend almost entirely on heroes alone . . . On the other hand, most comedy is certainly bisexual. We might search in vain among the thousands of our comedies to discover one single play wherein there was not at least one principal woman figure.'[33] Certain it is that the henpecked and outwitted male, from Chaucer and the Townely plays down to the modern comic strip, has been a constant prepossession of humorous writing.

In some respects the drastic inversion of the conventional pattern of sex behaviour is another aspect of Shaw's comic tilt against authority, represented in a patriarchal society by the ascendancy of the male. It is also, of course, another aspect of his perpetual war on romantic illusions, this time with ethereal maidens as its object. But Shaw pushes the inversion far beyond the normal usages of comedy. The woman does not merely outwit the man by superior guile and sham submission, or rule him through her tongue: she takes an unashamed initiative, often assumes the dominant role, and employs physical violence. It is in the relation between the sexes that an obtrusive farcical note, which critics usually find so irritating, is often sounded even in the major and more serious comedies. *Man and Superman* is the play which has as its main theme the pursuit of the helpless male by the predatory female; but Ann, as a deliberate satire on the 'womanly woman', is not typical of Shaw's heroines. She is outwardly compliant, and her

[31] *The Philanderer*, Act II, p. 43.
[32] George Meredith, *An Essay on Comedy*, 1903, pp. 28–9, 58–61.
[33] Nicoll, p. 46.

E

strategy and demeanour outrageously feminine. Yet even in *Man and Superman* a farcical note, manifested in a physical pursuit across Europe, is never far below the surface. Shaw seemed to take refuge in this extreme inversion to mask his inability, which he rationalized into a refusal, to treat of normal sexual attraction or sexual behaviour as a theme. Archer in writing of *Widowers' Houses* notes a deficiency which amounts almost to an abnormality:

> But however true to nature Blanche's tantrums may be, they are utterly irrelevant to this play. No doubt the daughter of a slum landlord *may* have a devilish temper, just as she may have epilepsy or a wooden leg; but there is nothing normal or highly probable in any of these peculiarities, whereas the artistic treatment of the theme obviously demanded that Blanche should be a normal girl, without any startling eccentricities. Her ferocity is a mere red-herring drawn across the logical trail, a disturbing and distressing irrelevance. . . . The full significance of this aberration of Mr. Shaw's was only to be revealed later, when we learned that he was merely yielding, on the threshold of his dramatic career, to an obsession from which he was hardly ever to escape. Himself the most even-tempered and self-controlled of men, he has somehow been induced to regard quarrelling, wrangling, jangling, scrapping and squabbling as the most dramatic element in life. Sheer ill-temper is, in the world he portrays, one of the mainsprings of human conduct.[34]

Elsewhere, Archer notes Shaw's predilection for 'violent love-making';[35] but although he remarks that it occurs in serious comedy,[36] he does not seem to have noticed that, while the men are often impetuous and precipitate, violence is usually the province of the women. The pronounced tendency towards an inversion of the sexes to be found in his early novels, which certainly have no humorous intent, suggests something more than a comic device, even to those who will have none of the machinations of psychoanalysis, with its sinister interrelation of wit with sadism and humour with masochism. ' "By Jingo!" exclaimed Cashel, with sudden excitement, "I dont care what you say to me. You have a way of giving things a turn that makes it a pleasure to

[34] William Archer, *The Old Drama and the New*, 1923, p. 346.
[35] *Ibid.*, p. 349.   [36] *Ibid.*, p. 349.

be shut up by you".'[37] The 'sudden excitement' reveals an erotic sub-ordination of beefy muscularity, in the Hercules–Omphale tradition, which colours a great part of *Cashel Byron's Profession*. Lydia chooses Cashel for his beauty, and Cashel is boyish and humble in her presence. 'He could only answer "Yes" in a constrained way, and stare helpless-ly and timidly at her.'[38] In *The Unsocial Socialist*, Sidney Trefusis in a mysteriously and voluntarily menial role is to be found kneeling before a row of young girls, who apparently wait for him to come and take their skates off one by one. 'If all the skates are off, I will by Miss Wil-son's order, carry them and the camp-stool back to the college.'[39] Elsewhere, Trefusis: 'You are the bright sun of my senses . . . I feel my heart and brain wither in your smile, and I fling them to you for your prey with exultation. How happy I am to have a wife who does not despise me for doing so—who rather loves me the more!'[40]

Examples could be multiplied; but it is enough to note that he seemed impelled repeatedly to express such a 'despicable' love, and persistently cloaked it in wild farce, the wilder the farce, the more extreme the subordination of the male. In the short farcical sketches, Shaw seems to give full dramatic licence to erotic fantasies. *The Music-Cure*, which he sub-titles as 'A Piece of Utter Nonsense', culminates in the follow-ing dialogue:

REGINALD. . . . Oh, Strega, dont you want a dear little domesti-cated husband who would have no concern but to please you, no thought outside our home, who would be unspotted and unsoiled by the rude cold world, who would never meddle in politics or annoy you by interfering with your profession? Is there any hope for me?

STREGA (*coming away from the piano*). My child: I am a hard, strong, independent, muscular woman. How can you, with your delicate soft nature, see anything to love in me? I should hurt you, shock you, perhaps—yes: let me confess it—I have a violent temper, and might even, in a transport of rage, beat you.

REGINALD. Oh do, do. Dont laugh at this ridiculous confession; but ever since I was a child I have had only one secret longing, and

---

[37] *Cashel Byron's Profession* (1882), Constable (standard edn.), 1950, p. 67.
[38] *Ibid.*, p. 216.
[39] *An Unsocial Socialist* (1883), Constable (standard edn.), 1950, p. 97.
[40] *Ibid.*, p. 66.

that was to be mercilessly beaten by a splendid, strong, beautiful woman.

. . . . . .

REGINALD. But you would be angry sometimes: terrible, splendid, ruthless, violent. You would throw down the thing you loved and trample on it as it clung to your feet.

STREGA. Yes—oh, why do you force me to confess it?—I should beat it to a jelly, and then cast myself in transports of remorse on its quivering frame and smother it with passionate kisses.

The Music-Cure, pp. 1130–1.

'Dont laugh at this ridiculous confession,' says Reginald. No, one does not laugh overmuch at *The Music-Cure*.

The Fascinating Foundling, sub-titled 'A Disgrace to the Author', describes the quest of Anastasia for a man she can bully, who, she says, is a necessity for her position 'as a woman'.[41] In *Great Catherine*, the comic highlight consists in Edstaston being tied up and being dumped at the feet of the Empress, who tortures him by tickling his ribs with her foot. We are left to infer that he enjoyed it, and that the treatment aroused the intense jealousy of Edstaston's betrothed.[42] In *Press Cuttings*, there are two prominent suffragettes: Mrs Banger, 'a masculine woman of forty with a powerful voice and great physical strength'[43] and Lady Corinthia, who is beautiful and romantic but uses a revolver.[44]

MRS BANGER (*to the Orderly*). When you are ordered to put a person out you should do it like this. (*She hurls him from the room. He is heard falling headlong downstairs and crashing through a glass door.*) I shall now wait on General Sandstone. If he shews any sign of weakness, he shall share that poor wretch's fate.

Press Cuttings, p. 1100.

Later General Sandstone proposes marriage to Mrs. Banger on the grounds that 'he has met his ideal at last'.[45]

In *Fanny's First Play*, Margaret, 'a strong, springy girl of eighteen,

---

[41] *The Fascinating Foundling*, p. 1124. [42] *Great Catherine*, Sc. IV, pp. 815–16.
[43] *Press Cuttings*, p. 1098. [44] *Ibid.*, pp. 1098–9.
[45] *Ibid.*, p. 1103.

with large nostrils, an audacious chin, and a gaily resolute manner', knocks out two of a policeman's teeth.[46] In *The Dark Lady of the Sonnets*, the Dark Lady, 'with two vigorous cuffs . . . knocks the pair asunder, sending the man, who is unlucky enough to receive a right-handed blow, sprawling on the flags'.[47] In *Too True To be Good*, the Patient is a violent woman who chases Aubrey, offering to kick him and beat him to jelly.[48] In *The Millionairess*, Epifania assaults Adrian with a straight left, a savage right, and knocks him downstairs with a mule kick.[49]

Such sex-propelled slapstick is presented with greater temperance in Shaw's more important works; but, as has been noticed in discussing *Man and Superman*, it often contributes a strangely extraneous and even discordant note. The irrelevant 'Interlude' in *The Apple Cart*, which ends up in a wrestling match between 'romantically beautiful' Orinthia and public-spirited King Magnus who lavishes public money on her, is dramatically idiotic. Orinthia is a fantasy, not a woman. Vivie Warren of *Mrs Warren's Profession*, with her iron handshake[50] and cigarette smoking,[51] may raise an easy laugh, but it defeats the purpose of Shaw's sermon if a woman has to be masculinised before she can pursue a career of her own. In *Getting Married*, an obtrusive farcical element is introduced in the relations between Hotchkiss and Mrs George, with violence threatened on both sides and the wrangle culminating in Hotchkiss kneeling at the feet of Mrs George, who seizes a poker and makes for him. He 'flies to the study door. The Bishop enters just then and finds himself between them, narrowly escaping a blow from the poker.'[52] Shaw sub-titles *Getting Married* as 'A Disquisitory Play'.

Shaw even shows a reluctance to subordinate women to those men who play a dominant role as the masters of reality and rise above the fate of ordinary men, helpless victims of women's procreative urge. In *Major Barbara*, Undershaft is extremely uncomfortable in going against an estranged wife's wishes in a matter which is vitally important to him. Shaw rescues him by making Stephen unwilling to go into the cannon business. How extraordinarily out of character is the armaments tycoon in the following dialogue:

---

[46] *Fanny's First Play*, Act II, p. 664.   [47] *The Dark Lady of the Sonnets*, p. 647.
[48] *Too True to be Good*, Act II, p. 1151.   [49] *The Millionairess*, Act II, p. 1267.
[50] *Mrs Warren's Profession*, Act I, p. 62.   [51] *Ibid.*, Act IV, p. 85.
[52] *Getting Married*, p. 580.

LADY BRITOMART. Andrew: you can talk my head off; but you cant change wrong into right. And your tie is all on one side. Put it straight.

UNDERSHAFT (*disconcerted*). It wont stay unless it's pinned (*he fumbles at it with childish grimaces*)——

Stephen comes in.

STEPHEN (*at the door*). I beg your pardon (*about to retire*).

LADY BRITOMART. No: come in, Stephen. (*Stephen comes forward to his mother's writing table.*)

UNDERSHAFT (*not very cordially*). Good afternoon.

STEPHEN (*coldly*). Good afternoon.

UNDERSHAFT (*to Lady Britomart*). He knows all about the tradition, I suppose?

LADY BRITOMART. Yes. (*To Stephen*) It is what I told you last night, Stephen.

UNDERSHAFT (*sulkily*). I understand you want to come into the cannon business.

STEPHEN. *I* go into trade! Certainly not.

UNDERSHAFT (*opening his eyes, greatly eased in mind and manner*). Oh! in that case——

LADY BRITOMART. Cannons are not trade, Stephen. They are enterprise.

STEPHEN. I have no intention of becoming a man of business in any sense. I have no capacity for business and no taste for it. I intend to devote myself to politics.

UNDERSHAFT (*rising*). My dear boy: this is an immense relief to me. And I trust it may prove an equally good thing for the country. I was afraid you would consider yourself disparaged and slighted. (*He moves towards Stephen as if to shake hands with him.*)

Major Barbara, Act III, p. 489.

Captain Brassbound's Conversion treats of the conversion of a male romantic by a female realist; and *Arms and the Man*, of the conversion of a female romantic by a male realist. The inferiority of the romanticist would therefore in both plays be in accordance with Shavian philosophy. But there is something very different from the submission of Brassbound to Lady Cecilia in Raina's relations with Bluntschli. Both extracts are from the last two or three hundred lines:

BRASSBOUND. . . . When you came, I took your orders as naturally as I took Gordon's, though I little thought my next commander would be a woman. I want to take service under you. And theres no way in which that can be done except marrying you. Will you let me do it?

Captain Brassbound's Conversion, Act III, p. 331.

BLUNTSCHLI (*to Raina, complacently*). I have put everything right, I hope, gracious young lady.

RAINA (*going to the table to face him*). I quite agree with your account of yourself. You are a romantic idiot. (*Bluntschli is unspeakably taken aback.*) Next time, I hope you will know the difference between a schoolgirl of seventeen and a woman of twenty-three.

BLUNTSCHLI (*stupefied*). Twenty-three!

Raina snaps the photograph contemptuously from his hand; tears it up; throws the pieces in his face; and sweeps back to her former place.

SERGIUS (*with grim enjoyment of his rival's discomfiture*). Bluntschli: my one last belief is gone. Your sagacity is a fraud, like everything else. You have less sense than even I!

Arms and the Man, Act III, pp. 121–2.

In *Pygmalion*, Eliza does not even marry Higgins, preferring, so Shaw explains carefully in the postscript, a lifetime of Freddy fetching her slippers to a lifetime of her fetching Higgins's.[53] Very different are the relations between Galatea Morell and his Pygmalion in *Candida*. Eliza throws his slippers at Higgins[54] and announces her complete independence, even threatening to set up a rival school of speech. 'Yes:' she says, 'you turn round and make up to me now that I'm not afraid of you, and can do without you.'[55] Morell, however, kneels beside Candida's chair and embraces her 'with boyish ingenuousness', saying: 'It's all true, every word. What I am you have made me with the labor of your hands and the love of your heart. You are my wife, my mother, my sisters: you are the sum of all loving care to me.'[56]

In Shaw's plays the theme of the ascendancy of women is used more persistently than in the plays of any other English writer. As a legitimate comic resource it gives good service: as a farcical expedient it leads him into regrettable extravagance.

[53] *Pygmalion*, Postscript, p. 753.
[55] *Ibid.*, Act V, p. 751.
[54] *Ibid.*, Act IV, p. 740.
[56] *Candida*, Act III, p. 151.

CHAPTER II

Types and Contrasts

THE presentation of a paradoxical theme as comedy requires a number of characters who represent the anomaly or disproportion under attack, as well as inverted characters and inverted situations. Sergius in *Arms and the Man*, Britannus in *Caesar and Cleopatra*, Ramsden and Octavius in *Man and Superman*, Walpole and B.B. in *The Doctor's Dilemma*, Broadbent in *John Bull's Other Island*, Stephen in *Major Barbara*, Freddie in *Pygmalion*, Boanerges in *The Apple Cart*, are a few examples of comic characters who are funny, not because they are inversions, but because they are exaggerations of the normal. They are the puppets of the system, the victims of romantic illusion in whom we find, as Bergson puts it, 'the manner seeking to outdo the matter, the letter aiming at ousting the spirit'[1] and whose rigidity of mind contrasts so strongly with the mental mobility of the vital realists. Bentley is probably indebted, as most modern writers on comedy must be, to the Bergsonian conception of the comic when he writes:

> The minor characters, on the other hand, are pure victims of system, existing in complete contrast to the vital heroes . . . This is one of the oldest comic contrasts. From the first, comedy has defended the human against that corruption of the human which takes place when a man comes to identify himself with his social function—of being a doctor, a soldier, a statesman, or even a son, a husband, a father. The Shavianizing of this perennially comic perception entails its absorption into vitalism and socialism.[2]

If, then, comedy satirises a system and does not merely make fun of individual eccentricities, it follows that the characters will be types, representing a particular aspect of that system:

> In one sense it might be said that all *character* is comic, provided we mean by character the *ready-made* element in our personality,

[1] Bergson, p. 53 (italicised).   [2] Bentley, *Shaw*, p. 170.

that mechanical element . . . Every comic character is a *type*. Inversely, every resemblance to a type has something comic in it.[3]

Thus, to depict characters, that is to say, general types, is the object of high-class comedy. . . . Not only are we entitled to say that comedy gives us general types, but we might add that it is the *only* one of all the arts that aims at the general; so that once this objective has been attributed to it, we have said all that it is and all that the rest cannot be.[4]

If the comic poet's object is to offer us types, that is to say, characters capable of self-repetition, how can he set about it better than by showing us, in each instance, several different copies of the same model?[5]

When a person is isolated in comedy he is nearly always a type, a representative of something broader than himself, and in the highest art a representative of what are the permanent classes of mankind.[6]

To be comic, on the other hand, a character must be seen as one unit in a society composed of other similar units. . . . The characters of comedy are not superhuman or subhuman, but on a level with the generality of mankind; and if they are eccentric their eccentricity is regarded as sheer misfortune, like a disease.[7]

The point of these quotations is to offset the frequent charge made against Shaw that his characters are types or puppets. All comic characters are puppets in so far as they preserve the outward and often dignified semblance of independent action but are really the unconscious creatures of habit and convention. And it is here that the criterion of inevitability as a component of the comic in the realm of sense makes its appearance. Inversion of character supplies the element of the unexpected, while the stereotyped and sclerotic characters supply the element of the inevitable. For just as nonsense is not funny unless it contains an element of sense, so is character not funny if it is completely unpredictable. The movements of a puppet are but very faintly amusing if they are aimless and meaningless, but they provide a comic spectacle if organised into a bizarre pattern in which a certain logic, however grotesque, can be seen. Perhaps, too, a sense of superiority, which is a

---

[3] Bergson, p. 148. [4] *Ibid.*, p. 149. [5] *Ibid.*, p. 165.
[6] Nicoll, p. 135. [7] Potts, p. 115.

fundamental reason why we find characters comic, must be satisfied in some degree by our being able to foresee how a character will behave in a certain situation. In brief, to be funny, a character must behave in character. Cokane in *Widowers' Houses*, Britannus in *Caesar and Cleopatra*, Broadbent in *John Bull's Other Island*, the Chaplain in *Saint Joan*, or any one of Shaw's other stereotypes of English stupidity, are funny because they are consistently stupid. If the Earl of Warwick had said, as the Chaplain said, that the saints Margaret and Catherine and the Archangel Michael would necessarily speak in English,[8] we should be repelled or puzzled, not amused—unless he was being ironical. If Broadbent's 'Yes: I know I have a strong sense of humor which sometimes makes people doubt whether I am quite serious'[9] were put into Larry Doyle's mouth, we should be perturbed at his fall from grace.[10]

The eccentricities of mind and character may reveal themselves in verbal repetition. In *Arms and the Man*, Sergius's 'I never apologise' is funny because he behaves 'like a repeating clock of which the spring has been touched'.[11] B.B.'s stimulation of the phagocytes and Walpole's blood poisoning through the nuciform sac in *The Doctor's Dilemma* become more laughable through repetition, as does Shotover's 'seventh degree of concentration' in *Heartbreak House*. Shaw, however, seldom uses and never overuses mere verbal repetition. Satiety, the greatest enemy of the humorist, can be reached very quickly in this primitive 'jack-in-a-box' type of humour; for the divorce from the unexpected becomes too complete.

In order that the expected and unexpected may be compounded into appropriate proportions it is also necessary for straight and comic characters to be judiciously intermingled. If every character is fatuous or egregious, then his appearances and behaviour bring rapidly diminishing returns. Such contrasts have already been noted in the interplay between the men of wit and their foils; the men of wit representing a desirable, although not necessarily an actual social norm, and the foils representing a comic deviation, either above or below the norm. It is not necessary, however, for the norm to be represented by a man of wit; although in drama it is more effective if it is represented in human form and does not remain a mere concept. In *The Doctors'*

---

[8] *Saint Joan*, Sc. VI, p. 992.   [9] *John Bull's Other Island*, Act IV, p. 444.
[10] Arthur Koestler in *Insight and Outlook*, 1949, p. 29, writes about inevitability as a criterion of comic technique, calling it the 'facilitation of the associative flow', which is determined to a large extent by 'the audience's mental habitus'.
[11] *Arms and the Man*, Act III, p. 120.

Dilemma, the gruff common sense of Sir Patrick and the sanity of Ridgeon supply the sense which makes the nonsense funny and throws up the charlatanism and pretensions of B.B. and Walpole into comic relief. It is illuminating to note how Shaw heightens the contrast in his stage directions, putting into practice the Bergsonian thesis that 'The attitudes, gestures, and movements of the human body are laughable in exact proportion as that body reminds us of a mere machine.[12] In Walpole and B.B. machine-like characteristics are emphasised, but Ridgeon and Sir Patrick are more than doctors—they are still men:

> Cutler Walpole is an energetic, unhesitating man of forty, with a cleanly modelled face, very decisive and symmetrical about the shortish, salient, rather pretty nose, and the three trimly turned corners made by his chin and jaws. In comparison with Ridgeon's delicate broken lines, and Sir Patrick's softly rugged aged ones, his face looks machine-made and beeswaxed; but his scrutinizing, daring eyes give it life and force. He seems never at a loss, never in doubt: one feels that if he made a mistake he would make it thoroughly and firmly.
>
> *The Doctor's Dilemma*, Act I, p. 509.

> Sir Ralph Bloomfield Bonington wafts himself into the room. He is a tall man, with a head like a tall and slender egg. . . . His fair eyebrows arch goodnaturedly and uncritically. He has a most musical voice; his speech is a perpetual anthem; and he never tires of the sound of it. . . . When he expands into oratory or scientific exposition, he is as energetic as Walpole; but it is with a bland, voluminous, atmospheric energy, which envelops its subject and its audience, and makes interruption or inattention impossible, and imposes veneration and credulity on all but the strongest minds.
>
> *Ibid.*, Act I, p. 510.

> Sir Patrick Cullen is more than twenty years older than Ridgeon, not yet quite at the end of his tether, but near it and resigned to it. His name, his plain, downright, sometimes rather arid common sense, his large build and stature, the absence of those odd moments of ceremonial servility by which an old English doctor some-

---

[12] Bergson, p. 29 (italicised).

times shews you what the status of the profession was in England in his youth, and an occasional turn of speech, are Irish; but he has lived all his life in England and is thoroughly acclimatized.

Ibid., Act I, p. 506.

Sir Colenso Ridgeon is a man of fifty who has never shaken off his youth. He has the off-handed manner and the little audacities of address which a shy and sensitive man acquires in breaking himself in to intercourse with all sorts and conditions of men. His face is a good deal lined; his movements are slower than, for instance, Redpenny's; and his flaxen hair has lost its lustre; but in figure and manner he is more the young man than the titled physician. Even the lines in his face are those of overwork and restless scepticism, perhaps partly of curiosity and appetite, rather than that of age. Just at present the announcement of his knighthood in the morning papers makes him specially self-conscious, and consequently specially off-hand with Redpenny.

Ibid., Act I, p. 505.

In the same way the doctrinaire dogmatism of the brigands in *Man and Superman* is both accentuated and prevented from becoming tedious by the clownish common sense of Mendoza. Indeed, in the earlier and greater comedies Shaw never makes the mistake of allowing eccentricity to dominate the stage. It was only later in his career when he had delivered his message and became impatient of the discipline imposed upon him by his art that a natural proclivity for farcical extravagance gained control. It is a long step from the Shaw of *Widowers' Houses* and *Mrs Warren's Profession*, when he found his themes so new and engrossing that he felt but little urge to transfigure them with his wit and humour, to the Shaw of such later plays as *The Millionairess*, *On the Rocks*, *Too True to be Good*, or even the *Apple Cart*, where there is such a preponderance of extravagant characters, such a repletion of rumbustious excess, that the comic balance between the inevitable and the unexpected is seriously upset. The unexpected has become the inevitable.

'The antithesis between Titania and Bottom is at the heart of comedy',[13] says Potts. But although in drama the comic antithesis or

---

[13] Potts, p. 25.

sustained anticlimax will obviously depend largely on the contrast of different characters, 'the dulness of the fool' is not the only 'whetstone of the wits'. Within us all there is both Bottom and Titania; and the comic antithesis may be found in single characters, in the difference between the character as he is and what he thinks he is, between his words and his deeds. In tragedy, inner conflicts are played out on an emotional and spiritual level, in comedy, on an intellectual and physical level. Tanner is not a figure of tragedy. He is a man of wit who degenerates into an almost comic character because the Superman within him succumbs to the Man. After his capitulation to Ann, the curtain falls on one of the most annihilating of all Shavian anticlimaxes:

> ANN (*looking at him with fond pride and caressing his arm*). Never mind her, dear. Go on talking.
> TANNER. Talking!
> *Universal laughter.*
>
> *Man and Superman*, Act IV, p. 405.

The pretensions of the intellect have been overcome by the demands of the body.

In *Arms and the Man*, Sergius exemplifies the same comic antithesis within a character even more obviously. Two minutes after his genuine preoccupation with the 'higher love', he is waxing amorous with Louka, the servant-girl. In the Epilogue to *Saint Joan*, the main comic antithesis is provided by the speed with which Joan's former enemies withdraw when there is a possibility of the sincerity of their protestations being put to test. In *Androcles and the Lion*, one of the funniest lines in the play is 'Boys: he's killed the lot',[14] marking as it does the surrender of Ferrovius, the muscular Christian, to the call of the belligerent flesh: the inevitable eruption of frailty, jack in the human paradox.

But sociological drama is only adventitiously concerned with the antithesis to be found within a single character. It is not so much concerned with inherited original sin as with social attitudes which have been acquired and can therefore be changed. Its main purpose is not to make the individual look ridiculous, but to make what he stands for look ridiculous. Indeed, Chesterton divided up great humorists into two categories, "those who love to see a man absurd and those who

---

[14] *Androcles and the Lion*, Act II, p. 700.

hate to see him absurd.'[15] He put Shaw into the second category. The generalisation is, of course, too neat and facile; but it can be said of Shaw that his main aim was to stop men looking ridiculous by curing them of mistaken, anti-social, and unrealistic attitudes. This involves the contrasting characters of proselytizer and proselyte; and we may here strengthen the defence against the charge that Shaw's characters are types, devoid of inner contradictions and inconsistencies, by saying not only that types are necessary to comedy but that they are doubly necessary to sociological comedy. If there is little duality in Shaw's characters it is because sociological comedy seeks to convert by wit, that is to say on an intellectual plane, and therefore is necessarily unaccompanied by the emotional conflicts to be found in other forms of drama. Such conversions come about once dialectical defence has broken down. A more legitimate criticism of Shaw would be that, after the intellectual conversion of a character has taken place, it seems to have too little effect on the deeper levels of the personality. Shaw's great dramatic shortcoming was that he was often more interested in the audience than in the characters. There are partial exceptions. Major Barbara is one, but it is significant that in her conversion the slings and arrows of wit have little part. Shaw is converting himself. In her he is both defendant and plaintiff, and he is in a state of emotional conflict.

It is not, then, in a portrayal of the duality in human nature that Shaw's genius consists. Perhaps that is more the province of humour, which perceives, accepts, and makes no attempt at conversion. Wit is more a method of analysis. Says Bergson: 'In the broader meaning of the word, it would seem that what is called wit is a certain *dramatic* way of thinking. Instead of treating his ideas as mere symbols, the wit sees them, he hears them and, above all, makes them converse with one another like persons. He puts them on the stage, and himself, to some extent, into the bargain.'[16] Shaw wittily goes a step further than Bergson in this view of characters as the personification of ideas, when he says that there are only two dramatic characters, 'the long-haired aesthete and the clown'.[17] The clown, of course, represents the real and the long-haired aesthete the ideal, the contrast between which, says Bergson, is the most common of all comic contrasts.[18] Equally obvious is it that Shaw's clowns, like Shakespeare's fools, are not

[15] Chesterton, p. 232.   [16] Bergson, p. 105.
[17] Quoted by Eric Bentley, *The Modern Theatre*, 1948, p. 100.
[18] Bergson, p. 127.

fools: it is the long-haired aesthetes who are the fools. Sense masquerades as nonsense, and unmasks the nonsense which masquerades as sense. The clown or wit is consciously funny, and the long-haired aesthete or butt is unconsciously funny. Of this fundamental contrast sufficient examples have been given in other contexts.

But it would be even more wrong to lend support to the frequently made accusation that this contrast represents a hard and fast cleavage, created by Shaw with clock-work precision, than it would be to claim that there is no duality in Shaw's characters. For although dramatic wit requires a framework of inevitability which the types provide, to be persistently successful comedy still demands frequent injection of the unexpected. And so it is that unreality has its doughty defenders as well as its men of straw. Quite apart, too, from the exigencies of wit, Shaw was too good a showman to promote one-sided contests. A host of far more evenly matched contestants than Sense and Nonsense do battle. Barbara in *Major Barbara* and Keegan in *John Bull's Other Island* are not exponents of nonsense; they stand for an order which is morally superior and therefore ultimately more intelligent than that of their opponents. Indeed Keegan has far more wit and intelligence than Broadbent, the egregious master of reality, who finally gains the day. Characterization in the plays shows that Shaw knew that truth was many-sided.

CHAPTER III

Wit and Truth

THE exercise of wit can easily lead, not to truth, but to that very rigidity and falsity which it attacks. Or it can degenerate into cynical carping and biting bigotry. But Shaw's love of truth and his clear-headedness prevented him from forcing his characters into a predestined groove. A 'romantic' like Saint Joan often turns out to have a greater grasp of reality than the 'realist' and, in pursuing her apparently subjective creed, often steers closer to the truth than the realist who measures his objectivity by social criteria, as the Earl of Warwick and the pillars of the Church do. Moreover, the revolutionary of today is the conservative of tomorrow; and the resolution of any conflict contains within it the seeds of fresh conflict. The spirit of Prometheus Unbound is not more, but less, free than the spirit of Prometheus Bound; and Shavian wit is on the side of the free, on the side of the vital:

ANDERSON (*between Judith and Richard*). Sir: it is in the hour of trial that a man finds his true profession. This foolish young man (*placing his hand on Richard's shoulder*) boasted himself the Devil's Disciple; but when the hour of trial came to him, he found that it was his destiny to suffer and be faithful to the death. I thought myself a decent minister of the gospel of peace; but when the hour of trial came to me, I found that it was my destiny to be a man of action, and that my place was amid the thunder of the captains and the shouting. So I am starting life at fifty as Captain Anthony Anderson of the Springtown militia; and the Devil's Disciple here will start presently as the Reverend Richard Dudgeon, and wag his pow in my old pulpit, and give good advice to this silly sentimental little wife of mine (*putting his other hand on her shoulder. She steals a glance at Richard to see how the prospect pleases him*). Your mother told me, Richard, that I should never have chosen Judith if I'd been born for the ministry. I am afraid she was right; so, by your leave, you may keep my coat and I'll keep yours.

RICHARD. Minister—I should say Captain. I have behaved like a fool.

JUDITH. Like a hero.

RICHARD. Much the same thing, perhaps. (*With some bitterness towards himself.*) But no: if I had been any good, I should have done for you what you did for me, instead of making a vain sacrifice.

ANDERSON. Not vain, my boy. It takes all sorts to make a world— saints as well as soldiers.

The Devil's Disciple, Act III, p. 249.

The reversal of roles is in both cases not accompanied by any emotional inner struggle. It is a spontaneous response to a new situation, perhaps too sudden to be completely convincing. But the sudden revelation of the paradox in man, the irruption of the unexpected into the inevitability of the type is the result of an intellectual approach, the approach of a man of wit who turns the tables on the 'realist' and transfers the dominant role to Anderson, who, by making the more effective and therefore more realistic approach, shows himself to be the more vital of the two.

LAVINIA. It meant more than that, Captain. It meant that a man cannot die for a story and a dream. None of us believed the stories and the dreams more devoutly than poor Spintho; but he could not face the great reality. What he would have called my faith has been oozing away minute by minute whilst Ive been sitting here, with death coming nearer and nearer, with reality become realler and realler, with stories and dreams fading away into nothing.

THE CAPTAIN. Are you then going to die for nothing?

LAVINIA. Yes: that is the wonderful thing. It is since all the stories and dreams have gone that I have now no doubt at all that I must die for something greater than dreams or stories.

THE CAPTAIN. But for what?

LAVINIA. I dont know. If it were for anything small enough to know, it would be too small to die for. I think I'm going to die for God. Nothing else is real enough to die for.

THE CAPTAIN. What is God?

F

LAVINIA. When we know that, Captain, we shall be gods ourselves.

Androcles and the Lion, Act II, p. 699.

The romanticism or idealism of Lavinia, unlike that of the Salva-
tionists in *Major Barbara*, is not just an Ibsenite façade hiding a grim
reality: it stands revealed as a deeper reality. The Captain himself seems
to realise that when he says 'By Great Diana, I think I would strangle
you if you gave in now.'[1] Nethercot says that this 'utterly humorless
imperialist officer begins to discard his false ideals and is well on the
road to becoming a humane realist himself as the curtain goes down.'[2]

B.B. (*coming between Louis and Walpole*). Twelve guineas? Thank
you: I'll take it at that. (*He takes it and presents it to Sir Patrick.*)
Accept it from me, Paddy; and may you long be spared to contem-
plate it.

SIR PATRICK. Thank you. (*He puts the drawing into his hat.*)

B.B. I neednt settle with you now, Mr Dubedat: my fees will
come to more than that. (*He also retrieves his hat.*)

LOUIS (*indignantly*). Well, of all the mean——! (*words fail him*) I'd
let myself be shot sooner than do a thing like that. I consider youve
stolen that drawing.

SIR PATRICK (*dryly*). So weve converted you to a belief in morality
after all, eh?

LOUIS. Yah!

The Doctor's Dilemma, Act III, p. 532.

The cat is suddenly transformed into the mouse. We have noticed
that a similar fate overtook Bluntschli in *Arms and the Man*, Higgins in
Pygmalion, and Tanner in *Man and Superman*. Here the reversal, although on a superficial plane, is symptomatic, not of the doctor's
dilemma, but of Shaw's dilemma. Who has the most claim to the
sympathy of a realist, the socially reprehensible Dubedat who is a
devotee of Art for Art's Sake, or the socially estimable Blenkinsop
whom Ridgeon elects to save in preference? Nowhere does Ridgeon
stand condemned for his decision; his defeat takes place only in the

---

[1] *Androcles and the Lion*, Act II, p. 699.

[2] Arthur H. Nethercot, *Men and Supermen*, Cambridge (Massachusetts), 1954,
p. 75.

significantly weak postscript of the fifth act when he seeks to marry the widow. Shaw may make a theoretical claim that the artist is not subject to a code of behaviour, but the playwright with a sociological purpose was not really comfortable in the doctrine.

DOYLE. . . . At last you get that you can bear nothing real at all: youd rather starve than cook a meal; youd rather go shabby and dirty than set your mind to take care of your clothes and wash yourself; you nag and squabble at home because your wife isnt an angel, and she despises you because youre not a hero; and you hate the whole lot round you because theyre only poor slovenly useless devils like yourself. (*Dropping his voice like a man making some shameful confidence.*) And all the while there goes on a horrible, senseless, mischievous laughter. When youre young, you exchange drinks with other young men; and you exchange vile stories with them; and as youre too futile to be able to help or cheer them, you chaff and sneer and taunt them for not doing the things you darent do yourself. And all the time you laugh! laugh! laugh! eternal derision, eternal envy, eternal folly, eternal fouling and staining and degrading, until, when you come at last to a country where men take a question seriously and give a serious answer to it, you deride them for having no sense of humour, and plume yourself on your own worthlessness as if it made you better than them.

John Bull's Other Island, Act I, pp. 411–12.

Perhaps nowhere does Shaw give more explicit utterance to his belief that wit, to remain on the side of the real, must remain on the side of the vital, and that there can be no hard and fast division between wit and truth on one side and seriousness and falsity on the other. To be always in the service of truth wit must retain the resilience of true intellectuality, otherwise it will degenerate into the laughter of the jackass or the sneering of one who does not believe in anything. Wit may be partisan and indulge in the half-truth for the purpose of exposing falsity, but it must remain conscious of its partisanship. In other words, it must have truth as its aim. Moreover, just as characters must have a degree of inevitability that comes from their being true to type if they are to excite mirth, so must what they say have the degree of inevitability that comes from its imparting some measure of truth if it is to be witty. The paradox, for example, is witty, not only because it is an unexpected truth, but because the truth, once seen, supplies the element of the inevitable, and 'pleasure is mixed with the blessed sensation of relief through recognition.'[3] 'How true,' says the audience, for even if they did not know it all the time they now imagine that they did. It is inevitability through repetition in a different guise, repetition of something that was already there even if not properly realised by the audience. 'Even where the design is malicious,' says C. E. Vulliamy, 'there is always an exposure of some fact or detail or essence which is undeniably true. Lacking this groundwork of truth, no satire is permanent or vital.'[4] He could have gone further and said 'permanent, vital, or amusing'.

The truth, however, does not necessarily have to be unexpected to be funny provided that the way it is presented is unexpected. 'Observation is the secret of the English Sense of Humour, which depends for its highest effects on the presentation of character by detail clearly and cleanly observed, so that hackneyed traits can be made to seem as fresh and memorable as a snowdrop, and worn-out old cabbage stumps of types, as distasteful as unwanted relatives from overfamiliarity, can spring into new life.'[5] Charlie Chaplain hardly did himself justice when he said that he made people laugh by 'telling them the plain truth of things'.[6] Nor did Will Rogers when he said 'I don't make jokes, I just watch the government and report the facts'.[7] E. B. White was nearer the truth when he said 'Humor at its best is a kind of heightened truth—a super-truth'.[8] It is heightened by the art with which it is presented. As Freud noted, 'the pleasure created by wit is dependent upon the technique on one hand and upon the tendency on the other hand. . . .'[9]

Shaw himself was, of course, very conscious that truth is a fundamental ingredient of wit. Chesterton even said that 'he will never admit of any of his jokes that it was only a joke. When he has been most witty he will passionately deny his own wit.'[10]

Twice in my life I have given prosaically truthful instructions to

---

[3] Potter, p. 164.   [4] C. E. Vulliamy, *The Anatomy of Satire*, 1950, p. 12.
[5] Potter, p. 164.
[6] Quoted by Max Eastman, *Enjoyment of Laughter*, New York, 1936, p. 273.
[7] *Ibid.*, p. 270.   [8] *Ibid.*, p. 270.   [9] Freud, p. 174.
[10] Chesterton, p. 158.

solicitors, and been surprised to find that they were not carried out. They thought I must be romancing or joking.

Sixteen Self Sketches, No. VIII, p. 43.

Many times he gave expression to the same point of view, twice, significantly enough, through the mouth of Keegan, one of his most sorrowful selfs:

KEEGAN. My way of joking is to tell the truth. It's the funniest joke in the world.

John Bull's Other Island, Act II, p. 418.

KEEGAN (*halting and turning to them for the last time*). Every dream is a prophecy: every jest is an earnest in the womb of Time.

Ibid., Act IV, p. 452.

And a paradox from Bluntschli, taken in its context, demonstrates the fusion of technique and truth in the formation of wit:

RAINA (*wonderingly*). Do you know, you are the first man I ever met who did not take me seriously?

BLUNTSCHLI. You mean, dont you, that I am the first man that has ever taken you quite seriously?

Arms and the Man, Act III, p. 113.

The proportions in which truth and technique are combined to produce the maximum effect cannot, of course, be measured. The ingredients of wit can no more be weighed in the balance than the capricious form and protean face of the final product can be photographed. It has already been said that truth is not in itself sufficient. Sometimes stark reality is very funny, for authenticity lends it the delight which comes from unaided recognition. The pleasure of coming across a *bêtise* or a boner in a piece of writing that purports to be serious is much greater than that of reading it in a prepared list of similar boners. But this is unconscious humour. For humour as an art, the act—as distinct from technique—of representation is necessary; and representation involves a change of context, which in its turn involves a change of attitude. Any practising humorist knows that people will laugh at a factual representation of drivel which they normally take seriously. Wordsworth defined poetry as 'emotion recollected in tranquillity'. Much humour is irritation recollected in tranquillity. Distance, imparted either by time or the indirection of art, is usually necessary for us to be able to laugh at the truth. When Bergson wrote that 'there are scenes in real life so closely bordering on high-class comedy that the stage might adopt them without changing a single word',[11] he was perhaps not taking into account what the very act of adoption entailed. If we admit as a definition of humour that it depends on the contrast between the loftiness of human aspirations or pretensions and the extent to which they are fulfilled, then perhaps stark reality is usually too funny and must be made less painful to excite laughter. Malcolm Muggeridge, like Will Rogers and Charlie Chaplin, is being humorous and not entirely truthful when he says that 'humour only exists in so far as it is truthful. The moment it departs from truth it is automatically transubstantiated into some *ersatz* product like whimsy.'[12] Comedians and men of wit are such serious-minded people that there is a strong tendency for them to magnify the serious part of their business, especially as that business is not by tradition and popular prejudice usually ranked so highly as other more obviously oracular branches of entertainment and literature.

If, too, wit and humour were the exclusive product of truth, then naturalism would be their obvious literary mode of expression; but in practice the more thoroughgoing naturalism becomes, the more harrowing and less witty it is. Shaw, himself a great admirer of Brieux, quickly abandoned the naturalistic technique, to be found in part in *Mrs Warren's Profession*, as his comedic talents began to develop. An illuminating contrast is between the unwitty but successful defence by Mrs Warren of her profession and the witty, more effective, but logically less successful defence by Undershaft of a far more gruesome profession. Mrs Warren deals in truth and is not witty. Undershaft deals in half-truth and is witty.

Betweene this [Falshood], and Truth, ly's the Proper Sphere of wit, which though it seeme to incline to falshood, do's it only to give Intelligence to Truth. For as there is a Trick in Arithmetique, By

---

[11] Bergson, p. 136.
[12] Malcolm Muggeridge, Foreword, *The Pick of Punch*, ed. Nicolas Bentley, 1956, p. 10.

giving a False Number, to finde out a True one: So wit by a certaine slight of the Minde, deliver's things otherwise than they are in Nature, by rendring them greater or lesse then they really are (which is cal'd Hyperbole) or by putting them into some other condition then Nature ever did. . . . But when it imploys those things which it borrows of Falshood, to the Benefit and advantage of Truth, as in Allegories, Fables, and Apologues, it is of excellent use, as making a Deeper impression into the mindes of Men then if the same Truths were plainely deliver'd.[13]

Shaw was a self-confessed dealer in half-truths. He said that it is necessary to 'exaggerate an ignored half-truth to the point at which it poses as a truth startling enough to shock people out of their complacency.'[14] He knew that 'consciousness of a fact is not knowledge of it'.[15]

> LADY UTTERWORD. . . . There are only two classes in good society in England: the equestrian classes and the neurotic classes.
>
> *Heartbreak House*, Act III, p. 795.

In this statement there is little truth, consigning, as it does, an even larger proportion of the English upper class to neurosis than Psychology does. It depends more for its success on technique, the loose construction emphasising the flippancy of the anticlimactic classification in contrast to the sociological pretensions of the climax. But, as Captain Shotover says, 'There is some truth in this'.[16] Adherence to tradition is a bulwark against neurosis.

> NURSE GUINNESS. . . . And very glad you should be to see your own daughter again after all these years.
>
> THE CAPTAIN. I am not glad. The natural term of the affection of the human animal for its offspring is six years.
>
> *Ibid.*, Act I, pp. 759–60.

---

[13] Samuel Butler, 'Miscellaneous Observations and Reflections on Various Subjects', *Characters and Passages from Note-books*, ed. A. R. Waller, Cambridge, 1908, p. 401; quoted by Ellen Douglass Leyburn, *Satiric Allegory: Mirror of Man*, New Haven, 1956, p. 38.

[14] Joad, p. 86.   [15] *Back to Methuselah*, Pt. IV, p. 919.

[16] *Heartbreak House*, Act III, p. 795.

The truth of the Captain's statement is more striking than that of Lady Utterword. It relies less on technique for its humour, the anti-climax to Nurse Guinness's fond and conventional expectation being far less sudden.

> CAPTAIN SHOTOVER. . . . Who are the men that do things? The husbands of the shrew and of the drunkard, the men with the thorn in the flesh.
>
> *Ibid.*, Act I, p. 774.

The truth of this statement is even more compelling than that of the second example; and technique in presentation is almost completely neglected, being limited to a climactic question to which, however, the answer is only unexpected if examined in a wider context. It does not come as a particularly sudden antithesis to the usual romantic idea that men owe their success to good wives.

The three examples have been arranged in descending order of funniness and in ascending order of truth in order to show that too much importance must not be attached to extravagant claims concerning the truthfulness of wit, and to show that the one containing the least amount of truth can make the greatest impact. It is not enough to tell the truth to people who are steeped in falsity.

Far more important than the verbal truth of a statement is the motive actuating the statement. A series of verbal truths may leave a false impression, and the chief means of distortion is not through the lie direct or the half-truth but through judicious omission. The half-truth is honest in its dishonesty; for in the half-truth the other half of the truth is implicit, and in drama, which thrives on conflict, it will often be explicitly stated. Two halves do make a whole, and, as has been pointed out, wit by its very nature must feed on both halves or die. It is the earnest absolutist, not the witty pragmatist, who builds up great systems of illusion or self-deceit. Not all the doctors in *The Doctor's Dilemma* are fakes and charlatans, and the picture of the medical profession that emerges is probably more truthful than the usual panegyrics which eulogise the triumphs of medicine and ignore its shortcomings. Similarly, especially if considered collectively, *Widowers' Houses*, *Mrs Warren's Profession*, *John Bull's Other Island*, and *Major Barbara* give a far more impartial presentation of the vices and virtues of the economic system than can be found either in socialist indictments or in capitalist vindications.

But perhaps more germane to the present study is the consideration that Shaw was writing plays and not indictments, vindications, or scientific expositions. He was using the half-truth as a rhetorical device which compels attention. Many of the characteristics of wit such as condensation, concreteness, absence of modifying clauses, sudden and poetic insight, purposeful omission, and paradox are also characteristics of the half-truth. Locke's view that 'in writings which aim at truth, all figurative expressions are "perfect cheats" '[17] would, if pushed to its logical conclusion, mean that art was divorced from life and could make no contribution to truth; for all art is figurative and interpretative. It makes the obvious less obvious and therefore more interesting; it makes the less obvious more obvious and therefore more arresting; and it reveals to those who can apprehend, all that cannot be discovered by ratiocination, caught by the camera, or expressed in expository and abstract language. 'And, Sir, as to metaphorical expression, that is a great excellence in style, when it is used with propriety, for it gives you two ideas for one; conveys the meaning more luminously, and generally with a perception of delight.'[18] If there is nothing new under the sun, it is the business of art to make it seem new. The moralist who observes that there is a decline in parental solicitude and affection as a child grows older may be more truthful than Shotover, but he is contributing less to the cause of truth and therefore to the sum of truth. And how long and tediously would a writer on political science dwell on the following theme:

> LORD SUMMERHAYS. Yes. Democracy reads well; but it doesnt act well, like some people's plays. No, No, my friend Tarleton: to make Democracy work, you need an aristocratic democracy. To make Aristocracy work, you need a democratic aristocracy. Youve got neither; and theres an end of it.
>
> *Misalliance*, p. 613.

Or an educationalist on the following:

> LORD SUMMERHAYS. Reading is a dangerous amusement, Tarleton. I wish I could persuade your free library people of that.

[17] Quoted by F. L. Lucas, *Style*, 1955, footnote, p. 201.
[18] *Ibid.*, quoting Dr Johnson, p. 218.

TARLETON. Why, man, it's the beginning of education.

LORD SUMMERHAYS. On the contrary, it's the end of it. How can you dare teach a man to read until youve taught him everything else first?

Ibid., p. 613.

'I use the metaphorical', said Meredith, 'to avoid the long-winded.'[19] Shaw used the half-truth for the same reason.

The half-truth, then, is a means of providing the sudden and unexpected element within the framework of the 'inevitability' of the truth. It is also the means of providing the other half of the truth, as the anticlimax to an unstated or stated climax. In other words, the anticlimax is also a half-truth, first correcting the excesses of the climax and then acting as its complement. It is the artist-wit's method of meeting the objection foreseen, of introducing provisos and qualifications without ruining the dramatic dialogue with modifying clauses, and of maintaining the loose constructions so favourable to his craft. Perhaps even more important, it is his means of maintaining an intellectual approach; of combating the tyranny of words; of puncturing the hyperbole with the understatement, the subjective with the objective, and emotionally charged rhetoric with common sense. 'From Milton to Ruskin, even to D. H. Lawrence, the Puritan had been the inebriate of verbal sound.'[20] But Shaw knew all about the evils of drink. 'He held many beliefs but he did not hold them as most of us do. He never appeared to be emotionally committed to them. He could advance or defend them without anger.'[21] Shaw hated moralising, moral indignation, and heroic postures.

THE MAN. . . . And here at last is their sentinel—an image of the constant and immortal part of my life, silent, full of thoughts, alone in the silver desert. Sphinx, Sphinx: I have climbed mountains at night to hear in the distance the stealthy footfall of the winds that chase your sands in forbidden play—our invisible children, O Sphinx, laughing in whispers. My way hither was the way of destiny; for I am he of whose genius you are the symbol: part brute,

---

[19] *Ibid.*, quoted, p. 206.

[20] V. S. Pritchett, *The English Puritan*, The New Statesman and Nation, Jan. 26, 1957, p. 104.

[21] J. B. Priestley, *Thoughts on Shaw*, The New Statesman and Nation, July 28 1956, p. 96.

part woman, and part god—nothing of man in me at all. Have I read your riddle, Sphinx?

THE GIRL (*who has wakened, and peeped cautiously from her nest to see who is speaking*). Old gentleman.

Caesar and Cleopatra, Act I, pp. 257–8.

Perhaps an even more shattering, although not so amusing, anti-climax comes some lines later:

CLEOPATRA. . . . . It is the moon that makes you talk to yourself in that silly way.

CAESAR. What! you heard that, did you? I was saying my prayers to the great Sphinx.

CLEOPATRA. But this isnt the great Sphinx.

CAESAR (*much disappointed, looking up at the statue*). What!

CLEOPATRA. This is only a dear little kitten of a Sphinx. Why, the great Sphinx is so big that it has a temple between its paws. This is my pet Sphinx.

Ibid., Act I, p. 258.

The episode, which has been criticized by those who imagine that Shaw is writing a play about a great romantic conqueror, sets the tone for the whole play with extraordinary skill. Shaw's anticlimaxes often have much more than an immediate significance.

PROTEUS. My friends, we came here to a meeting. We find, alas! that the meeting is to be a leavetaking. (*Crassus sniffs tearfully.*) It is a sad leavetaking on our part, but a cordial one. (Hear Hear *from Pliny.*) We are cast down, but not discouraged. Looking back to the past with regret, we can still look forward to the future with hope. That future has its dangers and its difficulties. It will bring us new problems; and it will bring us face to face with a new king. But the new problems and the new king will not make us forget our old counsellor, monarch, and—he will allow me to say— comrade. (Hear Hears *ad libitum.*) I know my words will find an echo in all your hearts when I conclude by saying that whatsoever king shall reign——

AMANDA. Youll be the Vicar of Bray, Joe.

The Apple Cart, Act II, p. 1041.

Lysistrata's 'She has a perfect right to speak. You are a parcel of senti-mental fools' a few lines later supplies an over-obvious explanation. But it is more than an isolated anticlimax; it is the preliminary setting of the stage for King Magnus's trump card, his return to politics as a commoner.

> BROADBENT. Of course I know that the moral code is different in Ireland. But in England it's not considered fair to trifle with a woman's affections.
>
> DOYLE. You mean that an Englishman would get engaged to another woman and return Nora her letters and presents with a letter to say he was unworthy of her and wished her every happiness?
>
> *John Bull's Other Island*, Act I, p. 415.

Doyle's statement is so near the truth that it would hardly be a witti-cism if it were not an anticlimactic interpretation of Broadbent's romantic patriotism. It is, of course, not very hilarious because it is lengthier than the preceding climax, and the demolition process is not complete until the last word.

> KEEGAN (*blandly*). That is not quite what occurred. (*He collects himself for a serious utterance: they attend involuntarily.*) I heard that a black man was dying, and that the people were afraid to go near him. When I went to the place I found an elderly Hindoo, who told me one of those tales of unmerited misfortune, of cruel ill luck, of relent-less persecution by destiny, which sometimes wither the common-places of consolation on the lips of a priest. But this man did not complain of his misfortunes. They were brought upon him, he said, by sins committed in a former existence. Then, without a word of comfort from me, he died with a clear-eyed resignation that my most earnest exhortations have rarely produced in a Christian, and left me sitting there by his bedside with the mystery of this world suddenly revealed to me.
>
> BROADBENT. That is a remarkable tribute to the liberty of con-science enjoyed by the subjects of our Indian Empire.
>
> *Ibid.*, Act IV, p. 440.

'Tom:' said Doyle to Broadbent, 'why do you select my most tragic moments for your most irresistible strokes of humor?'[22] The reason

[22] *John Bull's Other Island*, Act I, p. 412.

is not far to be found. *John Bull's Other Island* records the triumph of the numskull, and nonsense continually punctures tragic rhetoric, effectively undermining any tendency that the play might develop to degenerate into a nostalgic tragedy about the death of a fictitiously romantic Ireland.

> B.B. No; but why? Why? Because, my dear Sir Patrick, though the germ is there, it's invisible. Nature has given it no danger signal for us. These germs—these bacilli—are translucent bodies, like glass, like water. To make them visible you must stain them. Well, my dear Paddy, do what you will, some of them wont stain. They wont take cochineal: they wont take methylene blue; they wont take gentian violet: they wont take any coloring matter. Consequently, though we know, as scientific men, that they exist, we cannot see them. But can you disprove their existence? Can you conceive the disease existing without them? Can you, for instance, shew me a case of diphtheria without the bacillus?
>
> SIR PATRICK. No; but I'll shew you the same bacillus, without the disease, in your own throat.
>
> *The Doctor's Dilemma*, Act I, p. 511.

Sir Patrick's answer is a salutary reminder to a germ-ridden medical profession. But with its prefatory 'No' it is only anticlimactic in so far as it answers two rhetorical questions; for, as in *John Bull's Other Island*, there is no systematic attempt to puncture nonsense, the atmosphere that Shaw wishes to create being one that is favourable to charlatanism. Consequently, anticlimaxes are mild and are used merely to satisfy the exigencies of drama, the method of self-revelation being more suited to Shaw's purpose. B.B. continues as follows:

> B.B. No, not the same, Sir Patrick. It is an entirely different bacillus; only the two are, unfortunately, so exactly alike that you cannot see the difference. 'You must understand, my dear Sir Patrick, that every one of these interesting little creatures has an imitator. Just as men imitate each other, germs imitate each other. There is the genuine diphtheria bacillus discovered by Loeffler; and there is the pseudo-bacillus, exactly like it, which you could find, as you say, in my own throat.

SIR PATRICK. And how do you tell one from the other?

B.B. Well, obviously, if the bacillus is the genuine Loeffler, you have diphtheria; and if it's the pseudo-bacillus, youre quite well. Nothing simpler. Science is always simple and always profound. It is only the half truths that are dangerous. Ignorant faddists pick up some superficial information about germs; and they write to the papers and try to discredit science. They dupe and mislead many honest and worthy people. But science has a perfect answer to them on every point.

A little learning is a dangerous thing:

Drink deep; or taste not the Pierian spring.

Ibid., Act I, p. 511–12.

B.B.'s assertion that it is his opponents who are addicted to half-truths makes further anticlimactic half-truths superfluous.

Each separate play, considered as a whole, must be seen in the perspective afforded by the anticlimactic technique. Perorations are not ultimate but penultimate. Shaw wanted no part in the creation of infatuated idealogues who think that beneficent progress can be achieved by words. The endings of *Man and Superman*, *Saint Joan* and *Pygmalion* have already been discussed in other contexts. Nearly all the plays end on a sober note, flippancy often being a means of achieving sobriety:

BARBARA. Yes, through the raising of hell to heaven and of man to God, through the unveiling of an eternal light in the Valley of The Shadow. (*Seizing him with both hands.*) Oh, did you think my courage would never come back? did you believe that I was a deserter? that I, who have stood in the streets, and taken my people to my heart, and talked of the holiest and greatest things with them, could ever turn back and chatter foolishly to fashionable people about nothing in a drawing room? Never, never, never, never: Major Barbara will die with the colors. Oh! and I have my dear little Dolly boy still; and he has found me my place and my work. Glory Hallelujah! (*She kisses him.*)

CUSINS. My dearest: consider my delicate health. I cannot stand as much happiness as you can.

BARBARA. Yes: it is not easy work being in love with me, is it? But it's good for you. (*She runs to the shed, and calls, childlike.*) Mamma!

Mamma! (*Bilton comes out of the shed, followed by Undershaft.*) I want Mamma.

UNDERSHAFT. She is taking off her list slippers, dear. (*He passes on to Cusins.*) Well? What does she say?

CUSINS. She has gone right up into the skies.

LADY BRITOMART (*coming from the shed and stopping on the steps, obstructing Sarah, who follows with Lomax. Barbara clutches like a baby at her mother's skirt*). Barbara: when will you learn to be independent and to act and think for yourself? I know as well as possible what that cry of 'Mamma, Mamma,' means. Always running to me!

SARAH (*touching Lady Britomart's ribs with her finger tips and imitating a bicycle horn*). Pip! pip!

LADY BRITOMART (*highly indignant*). How dare you say Pip! pip! to me, Sarah? You are both very naughty children. What do you want, Barbara?

BARBARA. I want a house in the village to live in with Dolly. (*Dragging at the skirt.*) Come and tell me which one to take.

UNDERSHAFT (*to Cusins*). Six o'clock tomorrow morning, Euripides.

Major Barbara, Act III, p. 503.

Cusins was merely asking Barbara to moderate her egotistical and millennial transports, which is just what she does when she suddenly becomes a little girl dragging at her mother's skirts. 'Six o'clock to-morrow morning, Euripides' applies the closure on an even more practical note than the choosing of a house to live in. Not fine speeches nor histrionic climaxes but sweat and toil is the answer.

VIVIE. Yes: it's better to choose your line and go through with it. If I had been you, mother, I might have done as you did; but I should not have lived one life and believed in another. You are a conventional woman at heart. That is why I am bidding you good-bye now. I am right, am I not?

MRS WARREN (*taken aback*). Right to throw away all my money!

VIVIE. No: right to get rid of you? I should be a fool not to? Isnt that so?

MRS WARREN (*sulkily*). Oh, well, yes, if you come to that, I suppose you are. But Lord help the world if everybody took to doing the right thing! And now I'd better go than stay where I'm not wanted. (*She turns to the door.*)

VIVIE (*kindly*). Wont you shake hands?

MRS WARREN (*after looking at her fiercely for a moment with a savage impulse to strike her*). No, thank you. Goodbye.

VIVIE (*matter-of-factly*). Goodbye. (*Mrs Warren goes out, slamming the door behind her. The strain on Vivie's face relaxes; her grave expression breaks up into one of joyous content; her breath goes out in a half sob, half laugh of intense relief. She goes buoyantly to her place at the writing-table; pushes the electric lamp out of the way; pulls over a great sheaf of papers; and is in the act of dipping her pen in the ink when she finds Frank's note. She opens it unconcernedly and reads it quickly, giving a little laugh at some quaint turn of expression in it.*) And goodbye, Frank. (*She tears the note up and tosses the pieces into the waste-paper basket without a second thought. Then she goes at her work with a plunge, and soon becomes absorbed in its figures.*)

Mrs Warren's Profession, Act IV, p. 92.

Even Mrs Warren, after her tearful and ranting exhortations on the duties of a child to its mother, admits that Vivie is right. But the alternative to the repudiation of a mother and a prospective husband is not freedom and adventure but hard work.

LYSISTRATA. . . . But I am heartbroken at your not coming into the House with us to keep old England in front and lead a new Party against Breakages (*tears come into her eyes*).

MAGNUS (*patting her consolingly on the back*). That would have been splendid, wouldnt it? But I am too old fashioned. This is a farce that younger men must finish.

AMANDA (*taking her arm*). Come home with me, dear. I will sing to you until you cant help laughing. Come.

Lysistrata pockets her handkerchief; shakes the King's hands impulsively; and goes with Amanda. The King plunges into deep thought. Presently the Queen comes back.

THE QUEEN. Now Magnus: it's time to dress for dinner.

MAGNUS (*much disturbed*). Oh, not now. I have something very big to think about. I dont want any dinner.

THE QUEEN (*peremptorily*). No dinner! Did anyone ever hear of such a thing! You know you will not sleep if you think after seven o'clock.

MAGNUS (*worried*). But really, Jemima——

THE QUEEN (*going to him and taking his arm*). Now, now, now! dont be naughty. I mustnt be late for dinner. Come on, like a good little boy.

The King, with a grimace of hopeless tenderness, allows himself to be led away.

The Apple Cart, Act II, p. 1043.

There is promise of Lysistrata's recovery from her disappointment at Magnus's refusal to participate in the 'farce'. Comic songs will do the trick. The Queen, who has already been used as an antidote to Orinthia's romantic ravings, is once again pressed into service in much the same way as Major Barbara's mamma. Our last glimpse is not of Magnus, the political colossus, but of Magnus, the good little boy. Perhaps all humour depends in some measure on the injection of the objectivity of childhood into the pretensions of adulthood.

KEEGAN. In my dreams it is a country where the State is the Church and the Church the people: three in one and one in three. It is a commonwealth in which work is play and play is life: three in one and one in three. It is a temple in which the priest is the worshipper and the worshipper the worshipped: three in one and one in three. It is a godhead in which all life is human and all humanity divine: three in one and one in three. It is, in short, the dream of a madman. (*He goes away across the hill.*)

BROADBENT (*looking after him affectionately*). What a regular old Church and State Tory he is! He's a character: he'll be an attraction here. Really almost equal to Ruskin and Carlyle.

LARRY. Yes; and much good they did with all their talk!

BROADBENT. Oh tut, tut, Larry! They improved my mind: they raised my tone enormously. I feel sincerely obliged to Keegan: He has made me feel a better man: distinctly better. (*With sincere elevation*) I feel now as I never did before that I am right in devoting my life to the cause of Ireland. Come along and help me to choose the site for the hotel.

John Bull's Other Island, Act IV, p. 452.

As does Major Barbara, Keegan supplies his own anticlimax, which softens the typical Broadbent anticlimax that follows. The play must not be allowed to end on dreams, even if they are the dreams of a madman, nor must it end on the laughter of the jackass. Shaw does not end

G

his plays on a sudden and riotous anticlimax: there is a gradual stepping-down from the stage to the real world. Much good the moralising Ruskin and the grandiloquent Carlyle did with all their talk. Far more sensible to equate the cause of Ireland with the choosing of the site for a new hotel, with Keegan as an 'attraction', as a sideshow freak.

> CAESAR. Her sons. Come, Cleopatra: forgive me and bid me fare-well; and I will send you a man, Roman from head to heel and Roman of the noblest; not old and ripe for the knife; not lean in the arms and cold in the heart; not hiding a bald head under his conqueror's laurels; not stooped with the weight of the world on his shoulders; but brisk and fresh, strong and young, hoping in the morning, fighting in the day, and revelling in the evening. Will you take such an one in exchange for Caesar?
>
> CLEOPATRA (*palpitating*). His name, his name?
>
> CAESAR. Shall it be Mark Antony? (*She throws herself into his arms.*)
>
> RUFIO. You are a bad hand at a bargain, mistress, if you will swop Caesar for Antony.
>
> CAESAR. So now you are satisfied.
>
> CLEOPATRA. You will not forget.
>
> CAESAR. I will not forget. Farewell: I do not think we shall meet again. Farewell. (*He kisses her on the forehead. She is much affected and begins to sniff. He embarks.*)
>
> THE ROMAN SOLDIERS (*as he sets his foot on the gangway*). Hail, Caesar; and farewell!
>
> *He reaches the ship and returns Rufio's wave of the hand.*
>
> APOLLODORUS (*to Cleopatra*). No tears, dearest Queen: they stab your servant to the heart. He will return some day.
>
> CLEOPATRA. I hope not. But I cant help crying, all the same. (*She waves her handkerchief to Caesar; and the ship begins to move.*)
>
> THE ROMAN SOLDIERS (*drawing their swords and raising them in the air*). Hail, Caesar!
>
> *Caesar and Cleopatra*, Act V, pp. 296–7.

This extract is quoted as one of the most emotional of all the endings to Shaw's plays. But even Cleopatra's regret at Caesar's departure is not strong enough for her to wish for his return. Mark Antony will replace Caesar. Youth will replace age. The world will go on—the realist and vital world of the wit, not the illusory Utopia of the romantic.

CHAPTER IV

Irony

T O S A Y that wit nearly always deals in half-truths or that the sphere of wit lies between falsehood and truth is another way of saying that wit deals in understatement and overstatement, the plain statement being the non-witty expression of the truth. If the understatement and the overstatement become so extreme that they say the opposite of what is meant, then the field of irony and sarcasm, on a verbal plane at any rate, has been entered. Sarcasm might almost be described as exaggerated overstatement and irony as exaggerated understatement. Fowler's distinction between sarcasm, which works through inversion, and irony, which works through mystification,[1] obscures this fundamental identity of the two spheres of wit; but it does indicate that irony, like understatement, is usually a far more indirect and therefore artistic form of wit than overstatement or sarcasm. In sarcasm the inversion is obvious, but in irony it is decorous and disguised. The difference in relation between speaker and listener is fundamental.

Consequently, verbal irony is not suitable for the stage; for, as has already been remarked, the spoken word demands an immediate response from the audience. The small circle of initiates to which irony addresses itself will dwindle to the playwright and his secretary if the irony is so delicate that it takes more than a moment to recognise, for the audience has no more than a moment to spare. Furthermore, Shaw, as Potts says, is not addressing 'a public of aesthetes, scholars, or literary critics. The lack of "art" with which Ben Jonson reproached Shakespeare has been vindicated, and I have little doubt that Mr Shaw's will be vindicated too, when time has placed him in perspective'.[2] There was in Shaw, too, none of what Herbert Read calls that 'mean and

---

[1] H. W. Fowler, *A Dictionary of Modern English Usage*, second edition, revised by Sir Ernest Gowers, 1965, p. 253.
[2] Potts, p. 41.

esoteric spirit that lacks common understanding and sympathy', which makes irony 'more often the weapon of an exclusive egotism', and 'explains why it is used but sparingly by writers of true eloquence'.[3] For Shaw the stage was no cave of Delphi but a public rostrum.

Dramatic desiderata, polemical necessity, and personal predilection would, then, all lead us to expect little verbal irony in Shaw. What little we do find is usually either what is known as 'heavy irony', which is practically indistinguishable from sarcasm, or is underscored so thickly that it cannot be missed:

UNDERSHAFT (*hugely tickled*). You dont say so! What! no capacity for business, no knowledge of law, no sympathy with art, no pretension to philosophy; only a simple knowledge of the secret that has puzzled all the philosphers, baffled all the lawyers, muddled all the men of business, and ruined most of the artists: the secret of right and wrong. Why, man, youre a genius, a master of masters, a god! At twentyfour, too!

Major Barbara, Act III, p. 490.

The irony is so heavy that it does not even deceive Stephen, an uncommonly common denominator.

KEEGAN (*with polished irony*). I stand rebuked, gentlemen. But believe me, I do every justice to the efficiency of you and your syndicate. You are both, I am told, thoroughly efficient civil engineers; and I have no doubt the golf links will be a triumph of your art. Mr Broadbent will get into parliament most efficiently, which is more than St Patrick could do if he were alive now. You may even build the hotel efficiently if you can find enough efficient masons, carpenters, and plumbers, which I rather doubt. (*Dropping his irony, and beginning to fall into the attitude of the priest rebuking sin.*) When the hotel becomes insolvent (*Broadbent takes his cigar out of his mouth, a little taken aback.*) your English business habits will secure the thorough efficiency of the liquidation. You will reorganize the scheme efficiently; you will liquidate its second bankruptcy. . . .

John Bull's Other Island, Act IV, p. 450.

[3] Herbert Read, *English Prose Style*, 1928, p. 190.

Here the speaker himself provides an immediate corrective to his own irony, which might otherwise have escaped detection by one of the silliest of Shaw's Englishmen. In this and the following extract the stage directions supply an additional remedial measure:

> KEEGAN. Could you have told me this morning where hell is? Yet you know now that it is here. Do not despair of finding heaven: it may be no farther off.
> LARRY (*ironically*). On this holy ground, as you call it, eh?
> KEEGAN (*with fierce intensity*). Yes, perhaps, even on this holy ground which such Irishmen as you have turned into a Land of Derision.
>
> *Ibid.*, Act IV, p. 451.

Apparently even Keegan's vitriolic rejoinder does not make the irony obvious enough for Shaw and is preceded by Larry's 'as you call it, eh?'.

> LADY CICELY (*rising with the coat in her hands*). Oh! Oh!! Nothing will ever persuade me that you are as pigheaded as that.
> BRASSBOUND (*offended*). Pigheaded!
> LADY CICELY (*with quick, caressing apology*). No, no, no. I didnt mean that. Firm! unalterable! Resolute! Iron-willed! Stonewall Jackson! Thats the idea, isnt it?
> BRASSBOUND (*hopelessly*). You are laughing at me.
>
> *Captain Brassbound's Conversion.* Act II, p. 316.

The 'caressing apology' is delivered with a sledge-hammer, and Lady Cicely's irony is made obvious with five separate synonyms, 'Thats the idea, isnt it?', and a remarkable flash of insight from Captain Brassbound, who must have been put on his guard by the five exclamation marks. One of Shaw's failings was to point his verbal irony far beyond even the requirements of the stage.

> UNDERSHAFT (*with a reasonableness which Cusins alone perceives to be ironical*). My dear Barbara: alcohol is a very necessary article. It heals the sick——
> BARBARA. It does nothing of the sort.
> UNDERSHAFT. Well, it assists the doctor: that is perhaps a less ques-

tionable way of putting it. It makes life bearable to millions of people who could not endure their existence if they were quite sober. It enables Parliament to do things at eleven at night that no sane person would do at eleven in the morning. Is it Bodger's fault that this inestimable gift is deplorably abused by less than one per cent of the poor? (*He turns again to the table; signs the cheque; and crosses it.*)

Mrs Baines. Barbara: will there be less drinking or more if all those poor souls we are saving come tomorrow and find the doors of our shelters shut in their faces? Lord Saxmundham gives us the money to stop drinking—to take his own business from him.

Cusins (*impishly*). Pure self-sacrifice on Bodger's part, clearly! Bless dear Bodger! (*Barbara almost breaks down as Adolphus, too, fails her.*)

Undershaft (*tearing out the cheque and pocketing the book as he rises and goes past Cusins to Mrs Baines*). I also, Mrs Baines, may claim a little disinterestedness. Think of my business! think of the widows and orphans! the men and lads torn to pieces with shrapnel and poisoned with lyddite! (*Mrs Baines shrinks; but he goes on remorselessly*) the oceans of blood, not one drop of which is shed in a really just cause! the ravaged crops! the peaceful peasants forced, women and men, to till their fields under the fire of opposing armies on pain of starvation! the bad blood of the fierce little cowards at home who egg on others to fight for the gratification of their national vanity! All this makes money for me: I am never richer, never busier than when the papers are full of it. Well, it is your work to preach peace on earth and goodwill to men. (*Mrs Baines's face lights up again.*) Every convert you make is a vote against war. (*Her lips move in prayer.*) Yet I give you this money to help you to hasten my own commercial ruin. (*He gives her the cheque.*)

Cusins (*mounting the form in an ecstasy of mischief*). The millennium will be inaugurated by the unselfishness of Undershaft and Bodger. Oh be joyful! (*He takes the drumsticks from his pockets and flourishes them.*)

Mrs Baines (*taking the cheque*). The longer I live the more proof I see that there is an Infinite Goodness that turns everything to the work of salvation sooner or later. Who would have thought that any good could have come out of war and drink? And yet their profits are brought today to the feet of salvation to do its blessed work. (*She is affected to tears.*)

JENNY (*running to Mrs Baines and throwing her arms around her*). Oh dear! how blessed, how glorious it all is!

CUSINS (*in a convulsion of irony*). Let us seize this unspeakable moment. Let us march to the great meeting at once. Excuse me just an instant. (*He rushes into the shelter. Jenny takes her tambourine from the drum head.*)

MRS BAINES. Mr Undershaft: have you ever seen a thousand people fall on their knees with one impulse and pray? Come with us to the meeting. Barbara shall tell them that the Army is saved, and saved through you.

Major Barbara, Act II, pp. 484–5.

Barbara's 'It does nothing of the sort'; Cusins's 'Pure self-sacrifice on Bodger's part'; Undershaft's widows, orphans, and shattered soldiers; Cusins's 'The millennium will be inaugurated by the unselfishness of Undershaft and Bodger', all add weight to the verbal irony, which would be sinking under its own ballast in any literary medium other than the drama.

But the passage contains much more than verbal irony. It is the very stuff out of which drama is made. Undershaft and Cusins, ironists both, look through the simple world of Mrs Baines and Barbara into the complex reality below. This complexity is best revealed in drama because complexity is often revealed by means of conflict; and conflict depends on the juxtaposition of opposites, which in its turn gives rise to an ironic antithesis sustained long enough to ensure a response from the audience. Mrs Baines and even Barbara are simple souls who live in the Fool's Paradise of their own immediate preoccupation. Undershaft and Cusins know that there is no Paradise except that of the Fool. The skulls of human beings struck down by Drink and War appear, not on Undershaft's but on Mrs Baines's shoulder, and supply their own grinning commentary.

Undershaft's defence is an inverted attack, an attack on sentimental evasion and Ibsenite 'idealism', the inversion being achieved by allying Guns and Alcohol with Salvation, ideas which in the creed of the romantic are antagonistic to each other. Such 'defences' are one of the commonest weapons of the ironist.

CROFTS (*after a stare: not at all displeased and much more at his ease on these frank terms than on their former ceremonious ones*). Ha! ha! ha!

ha! Go it, little missie, go it: it doesnt hurt me and it amuses you. Why the devil shouldnt I invest my money that way? I take the interest on my capital like other people: I hope you dont think I dirty my own hands with the work. Come! you wouldnt refuse the acquaintance of my mother's cousin the Duke of Belgravia because some of the rents he gets are earned in queer ways. You wouldnt cut the Archbishop of Canterbury, I suppose, because the Ecclesiastical Commissioners have a few publicans and sinners among their tenants. Do you remember your Crofts scholarship at Newnham? Well, that was founded by my brother the M.P. He gets his 22 per cent out of a factory with 600 girls in it, and not one of them getting wages enough to live on. How d'ye suppose they manage when they have no family to fall back on? Ask your mother. And do you expect me to turn my back on 35 per cent when all the rest are pocketing what they can, like sensible men? No such fool! If youre going to pick and choose your acquaintances on moral principles, youd better clear out of this country, unless you want to cut yourself out of all decent society.

. . . . . .

CROFTS (*with serious friendliness*). To be sure you did. You wont find me a bad sort: I dont go in for being superfine intellectually; but Ive plenty of honest human feeling; and the old Crofts breed comes out in a sort of instinctive hatred of anything low, in which I'm sure youll sympathize with me. Believe me, Miss Vivie, the world isnt such a bad place as the croakers make out. As long as you dont fly openly in the face of society, society doesnt ask any inconvenient questions; and it makes precious short work of the cads who do. There are no secrets better kept than the secrets everybody guesses. In the class of people I can introduce you to, no lady or gentleman would so far forget themselves as to discuss my business affairs or your mother's. No man can offer you a safer position.

VIVIE (*studying him curiously*). I suppose you really think youre getting on famously with me.

CROFTS. Well, I hope I may flatter myself that you think better of me than you did at first.

Mrs Warren's Profession, Act III, p. 83.

Crofts, like Gulliver in *Gulliver's Travels* and unlike Undershaft, is an unconscious ironist, his vindication of self and society being an unconscious attack on both. At first the defence is direct and almost truculent; but, as his confidence develops, it becomes more strongly ironical because his praise damns deeper and deeper and because his confidence is entirely misplaced. Irony is always satirical in intent; its main functions are self-revelation and exposure of social evils. Both are achieved through somebody's assumption that God is in His Heaven and all's right with the world.

> LICKCHEESE. Come, Mr Sekketerry: you and me, as married men, is out of the unt as far as young ladies is concerned. I know Miss Blanche: she has her father's eye for business. Explain this job to her; and she'll make it up with Dr Trench. Why not have a bit of romance in business when it costs nothing? We all have our feelins: we aint mere calculatin machines.
>
> *Widowers' Houses*, Act III, p. 26.

Lickcheese defends romance by poisoning its source.

> BURGE. Nonsense! That notion about the Church being unprogressive is one of those shibboleths that our party must drop. The Church is all right essentially. Get rid of the establishment; get rid of the bishops; get rid of the candlesticks; get rid of the 39 articles; and the Church of England is just as good as any other Church; and I dont care who hears me say so.
>
> *Back to Methuselah*, Part II, p. 878.

Burge's generous defence of the Church of England cuts away most of the grounds on which it could be attacked.

> THE LADY. Oh, I know, I know. How shamefully you have been treated! What ingratitude! But the country is with you. The women are with you. Oh, do you think all our hearts did not throb and all our nerves thrill when we heard how, when you were ordered to occupy that terrible quarry in Hulluch, and you swept into it at the head of your men like a sea-god riding on a tidal wave, you suddenly sprang over the top shouting 'To Berlin! Forward!'; dashed at the German army single-handed; and were cut off and made prisoner by the Huns.

AUGUSTUS. Yes, madam; and what was my reward? They said I had disobeyed orders, and sent me home. Have they forgotten Nelson in the Baltic? Has any British battle ever been won except by a bold individual initiative? I say nothing of professional jealousy: it exists in the army as elsewhere; but it is a bitter thought to me that the recognition denied me by my own country—or rather by the Radical cabal in the Cabinet which pursues my family with rancorous class hatred—that this recognition, I say, came to me at the hands of an enemy—of a rank Prussian.

THE LADY. You dont say so!

AUGUSTUS. How else should I be here instead of starving to death in Ruhleben? Yes, madam: The Colonel of the Pomeranian regiment which captured me, after learning what I had done, and conversing for an hour with me on European politics and military strategy, declared that nothing would induce him to deprive my country of my services, and set me free. I offered, of course, to procure the release in exchange of a German officer of equal quality; but he would not hear of it. He was kind enough to say he could not believe that a German officer answering to that description existed. (*With emotion.*) I had my first taste of the ingratitude of my own country as I made my way back to our lines. A shot from our front trench struck me in the head. I still carry the flattened projectile as a trophy. (*He throws it on the table; the noise it makes testifies to its weight.*) Had it penetrated to the brain I might never have sat on another Royal Commission. Fortunately we have strong heads, we Highcastles. Nothing has ever penetrated to our brains.

Augustus Does His Bit, p. 843–4.

It seems not inappropriate to end a consideration of irony as inverted attack with an example so extreme that, even on the stage, it must provoke a belly-laugh. Such a farcical defence and such ludicrous self-revelation, made possible by the extreme stupidity of Augustus, is unfortunately only legitimate and permissible in a light-hearted piece of tomfoolery.

But, as already indicated in dealing with rhetoric in Shaw, and with the passage in which Undershaft and Mrs Baines are involved, it is mainly through the juxtaposition of characters that drama dispenses its ironic contrasts and reveals that man's claim to be a creature guided by reason is a ridiculous and unsubstantiated pretension. The classic contrast is, of course, between the Eiron and the Alazon. 'This is the confrontation in the earliest Greek comedy of the Ironist and the Impostor, the Ironist in Shaw being always the soft-spoken vital man in harmony with himself, the Impostor being the professional man who has ideologies and habits instead of ideas and impulses.'[4] Here Bentley once again makes an application of Bergson's thesis that rigidity of mind is the chief target of comic criticism. The Eiron eschews emotion, and in doing so achieves the intellectual detachment necessary for the exercise of wit. In the Alazon, however, emotional and inflexible patterns conditioned by false social ideals take precedence over the intellect. The Eiron is placid, polite and deprecatory; while the Alazon is energetic, bombastic, and dogmatic. The Alazon is raised by his opponent's humility to a higher perch where he may be more easily attacked, and from which his fall is correspondingly greater.

But in drama, particularly in sociological drama, the same degree of detachment as we find in a Socratic *ingénu* or in a propitiatory Chaucer is not practicable. Self-speaking truth is no more possible than a too highly polished verbal irony. Some character or characters must speak the truth, and so it is only in the expository stage of the play, before the conflict has been joined, that the Eiron can be his anaemic self. As Worcester says in *The Art of Satire*, 'Irony delights in the collision of opposites' but it also 'offers a way of escaping from the conflict and rising above it'.[5] Bentley's 'soft-spoken' ironist is too great a simplification and, as has already been seen, the Undershaft of the beginning of the play is not the Undershaft of a later period. It is the vital man who has the gift of the gab, who is the master of rhetoric. Only if the vitalist is not primarily engaged in converting to realism but is converting from romanticism does he assume a mask of ironic diffidence.[6] Says Freud of Falstaff: 'Sir John's own humor really emanates from the superiority of an ego which neither his physical nor his moral defects can rob of its joviality and security.'[7] And it is this inner assurance, often expressing itself in alazonic joviality and pugnacity, which animates the so-called ironists of Shaw. There is none of the 'understating of the whole personality'[8] which Worcester notes in Socratic irony. The triumph of the ironist who is in part impostor is paralleled in the play, inevitable in its outcome and unexpected in its wit.

[4] Bentley, *Shaw*, p. 171. [5] Worcester, p. 141. [6] See p. 27.
[7] Freud, Footnote, p. 377. [8] Worcester, p. 95.

Andrew Undershaft comes in. All rise. Lady Britomart meets him in the middle of the room behind the settee.

Andrew is, on the surface, a stoutish, easy-going elderly man, with kindly patient manners, and an engaging simplicity of character. But he has a watchful, deliberate, waiting, listening face, and formidable reserves of power, both bodily and mental, in his capacious chest and long head. His gentleness is partly that of a strong man who has learnt by experience that his natural grip hurts ordinary people unless he handles them very carefully, and partly the mellowness of age and success. He is also a little shy in his present very delicate situation.

Major Barbara, Act I, p. 466.

In spite, perhaps, of Shaw's intentions, Undershaft's 'kindly patient manners' last no longer than it takes him to make the acquaintance of his family. He defends his profession as 'a profiteer in mutilation and murder'[9] with unironic energy and throws down the gauntlet to Barbara almost immediately.

UNDERSHAFT. May I ask have you ever saved a maker of cannons?

BARBARA. No. Will you let me try?

UNDERSHAFT. Well, I will make a bargain with you. If I go to see you tomorrow in your Salvation Shelter, will you come the day after to see me in my cannon works?

BARBARA. Take care. It may end in your giving up the cannons for the sake of the Salvation Army.

UNDERSHAFT. Are you sure it will not end in your giving up the Salvation Army for the sake of the cannons?

Ibid., Act I, p. 469.

Scarcely Socratic in method or manner. Indeed Shaw seems to feel the necessity for a more minor character, Cusins, to supply an ironic commentary on Undershaft.

In *Man and Superman*, Tanner is almost completely alazon in manner, mien, and conduct.

He is prodigiously fluent of speech, restless, excitable (mark the snorting nostril and the restless blue eye, just the thirty-secondth

<hr />

[9] *Major Barbara*, Act I, p. 468.

of an inch too wide open), possibly a little mad. He is carefully dressed, not from the vanity that cannot resist finery, but from a sense of the importance of everything he does which leads him to make as much of paying a call as other men do of getting married or laying a foundation stone. A sensitive, susceptible, exaggerative, earnest man: a megalomaniac, who would be lost without a sense of humor.

Man and Superman, Act I, p. 335.

It is not an attitude of ironic detachment, but this Falstaffian sense of humour and superiority of ego that makes of Tanner a Shavian man of wit. Ann fills the same role as Cusins in *Major Barbara*, finally imposing her matrimonial terms on Tanner as Cusins imposed his financial terms on Undershaft.

Higgins in *Pygmalion* is 'careless about himself and other people, including their feelings', and his 'manner varies from genial bullying when he is in a good humor to stormy petulance when anything goes wrong'.[10] In *Caesar and Cleopatra*, as has been seen, Caesar, the vitalist, starts off with a most rhetorical, undetached, unironical speech and is addressed by Cleopatra as 'Old Gentleman'.[11] Sartorius in *Widowers' Houses* is of an 'incisive, domineering utterance and imposing style . . . formidable to servants, not easily accessible to anyone'.[12] In *The Devil's Disciple*, Richard Dudgeon, the vitalist, wears an expression that is 'reckless and sardonic', his manner is 'defiant and satirical, his dress picturesquely careless'.[13] He makes an unironic début on the stage by insulting about five people.

Bentley's application of the classic comic contrast to Shaw is, then, more valid when the realist is engaged in the more negative task of converting not to realism but from romanticism, as in *Arms and the Man* with Bluntschli in opposition to Sergius and Raina, or in *Captain Brassbound's Conversion* with Lady Cicely in opposition to Brassbound. In *The Apple Cart*, too, the classic pattern has been exploited with great consistency. Even after the expository stage, in which Magnus makes a fool of Boanerges, the gullible alazon, when Proteus, a more worthy opponent, appears to do battle, Magnus maintains his assumption of ironic detachment. *Arms and the Man* is successful because it contains so many of the ingredients of drawing-room comedy, but *The Apple*

[10] *Pygmalion*, Act II, p. 721. [11] See pp. 80–1.
[12] *Widowers' Houses*, Act I, p. 2. [13] *The Devil's Disciple*, Act I, p. 224.

Cart and *Captain Brassbound's Conversion* are less successful on the stage. In both Magnus and Lady Cicely there is too much of the ironic detachment which arises from their negative and undramatically defensive positions. Thus is the scale tipped too heavily in favour of the inevitable at the expense of dramatic conflict, which, to be effective, requires a stronger injection of the unexpected.

No attention has yet been paid to the irony that springs from the conflict of the individual with his circumstances. These circumstances may depend merely on the contrivance of an immediate situation, all or some of the actors being in ignorance of a state of affairs with which the audience is, however, familiar. In Shaw, who despised or affected to despise the trivialities of plot, we should expect to find but little of this manipulated type of irony. In *Arms and the Man*, the action is based largely on the ignorance of many of the characters of Bluntschli's first-act irruption into Raina's bedroom, but in all the rest of Shaw's plays the audience seldom knows more about the true facts of a situation than practically every actor on the stage. A further weakness of *The Apple Cart* is that the conflict is resolved, not through force of argument but by a sudden *coup* with Magnus suddenly trumping the Prime Minister's ace. If the audience could have seen this card sticking out of Magnus's sleeve, the developing irony of the situation would probably have made it a better play. But Shaw would not, or could not, make use of the ordinary dramatic irony of situation.

When the circumstances with which the individual finds himself in conflict are not merely those of the immediate situation but of his whole way of life, there arises a profounder type of irony such as has already been noticed in the Salvation Army refuelling with Bodger's whisky. There is this form of irony, too, in *Widowers' Houses* when Trench, after his condemnation of Sartorius, finds that his own income is equally tainted. There is irony in *Captain Brassbound's Conversion* when the Captain finds that his own moral position is little better than that of the man whom he is pursuing with righteous vengeance. There is irony in *Androcles and the Lion* when Spintho finds he is more afraid of being eaten by lions than going to Hell, but in the end suffers both. But in each example it is not dramatic irony. The audience knows no more about the equivocal position of the victim than the victim himself. Shaw's audience does not consist of the ironist's circle of initiates watching the character acting in ignorance of his own condition: it is made up of romantics who must also suffer conversion. The irony consists in the audience, as well as the stage characters, being hoist with their own petards.

An even profounder level of irony arises from the contemplation of the individual in conflict, not merely with his own way of life, but with life itself. He is at odds with something over which he has no control, over which no control is apparently possible. He is at odds with the limitations imposed on him by his own mortality; he is at odds with an organic society with its own laws of development and decay, whose ends are as impossible to shape as those of the individual organism. Confronted with this spiritual *impasse*, the ironist admits defeat, withdraws to the sidelines and watches the efforts of others to conquer or compromise with amused and even flippant detachment. The philosopher, on the other hand, seeks to escape, less by shaping individual ends, than by gathering them up into a higher synthesis. The contradiction that is Shaw can only be understood if one sees in him both the flippant ironist and the philosopher, who would overcome both the shortcomings of our finite lives and our corrupt society through the higher synthesis of Creative Evolution, which was, by its very remoteness in time, a doctrine of immediate despair. And for this understanding a brief excursion into Shaw's thought and character is necessary.

CHAPTER V

The Springs of Wit

I. THOUGHT

THE relation between wit and thought is one aspect of the more general relation between form and content. In its hostility to mere virtuosity and dilettantism, criticism usually emphasises the primacy of content over form, of matter over mould. Certain it is that, as has already been seen with the predominance of sense over sound, form cannot achieve significance until meaning has been understood; and, despite those who maintain that it is not necessary to share an artist's convictions to appreciate his work to the full, it seems equally certain that a work of art makes a greater impact where there is identity of belief. Indeed, the recent decline in Shaw's reputation is perhaps partly attributable to the change in intellectual climate from rebellion to traditionalism. But an acknowledgement of the primacy of content need not take us so far as to claim, particularly in literature, that form is inherent in matter. Nor is any mechanical synthesis possible. We not only say what we believe but believe what we say, especially if we have said it well. The saying it well implies a successful technique, and a technique has an uncomfortable habit of gaining control over the technician. A whole new ethos can arise from a successful or even temporarily successful adaptation, and in literature a way of thought will be profoundly influenced by the form of presentation. The connection between wit, with its intellectual orientation, and thought is particularly close. Wit depends for its exercise on norms and standards of conduct and is difficult to evaluate as an independent entity. As Freud says, 'sometimes we overvalue the quality of the wit on account of our admiration for the thought contained therein, and then again we overestimate the value of the thought on account of the pleasure afforded us by the witty investment.'[1] Wit, then, is both cause and effect. And it is a technique

[1] Freud, p. 202.

that can act as a means of revelation and distortion at the same time.

Nor may the strong subjective element present in the exercise of wit be ignored. Both form and content are the outcome of the artist's attempt to achieve inner harmony by establishing a state of equilibrium between himself and society. The polemical writer does not simply choose his ideology; it also chooses him. The artist, who is also a polemical writer in so far as he seeks sympathy or conversion, does not simply choose his technique; it also chooses him. Both the intellect and its overt expression can only be fully understood against the background of feeling. That our most rational moments are influenced by irrational and unconscious forces is a truism of modern psychology. To say that these forces reveal themselves more in the work of the artist than in that of the scientist or logician is to say, not only that art reveals another aspect of truth, but that it also lays bare the soul of the artist. As critics have pointed out, Shaw, the polemical writer, often says things which Shaw, the playwright, finds are not so. The polemical writer says what he thinks; the playright says what he feels.

Literary criticism is, of course, almost by definition more interested in symptoms than the state of mind that gave rise to the symptoms; but in its natural revulsion from the jargon, simplifications, and wearisome ubiquity of psychology, it should remember that 'critics often misinterpret, because they simply do not know enough of human beings.'[2] In other words, not only do symptoms throw light on origins, but origins throw light on symptoms; and in discussing Shaw's wit, some mention must be made of the forces that shaped that wit. Such a survey, necessarily brief in a book devoted to Shaw's wit and satire,[3] should, however, be undertaken without talking more than can be helped about the unconscious. A man with a mind like Shaw's knew far more about himself than anybody else can ever know. 'For wit does not have recourse to compromise as does the dream, nor does it evade the inhibition.'[4]

But while the static treatment accorded Shaw by most writers is misleading, it must be remembered that although there will be talk of 'periods' and 'stages' and the use of two or three psychological terms, such facile dispositions and diagnoses should be applied to anything

[2] F. L. Lucas, *Literature and Psychology*, 1951, p. 15.

[3] For a fuller treatment of Shaw's political and philosophical development the reader is referred particularly to William Irvine, *The Universe of G.B.S.*, New York, 1949, and to Edmund Wilson, *The Triple Thinkers*, London, 1952.

[4] Freud, p. 274.

H

so organic as a life-work with becoming diffidence. Evolution of any kind is but a partial process. The old Adam is always lurking in the background.

The old Adam in Shaw's political life was, amongst other things, a socialist. With Shavian over-emphasis, Frank Harris remarks 'without his Socialism there would have been no Shaw, nor Shavian plays'.[5] John Parker, Chairman of the Fabian Society, speaks of the 'essential Bernard Shaw', the Shaw who 'was a socialist mainly interested in changing human society';[6] while Shaw himself said that 'the years from 1884, when the Fabian Society was founded, to the slump in Socialism which preceded the South African war, were the most honorable and enjoyable of his life.'[7] That the cerebral Shaw should make use of such affective words as 'honorable' and 'enjoyable' in talking of himself of all people, is suggestive of a longing for the past and penitence for the present.

His early socialism was revolutionary in temper. In the Fabian Manifesto of 1884, written by Shaw, he says: 'That we had rather face a Civil War than such another century of suffering as the present one has been.'[8] The day of November 13th, 1887, seems to have marked a point of departure. He himself took to his heels when a Trafalgar Square demonstration clashed with the police. From then onwards violence was renounced, and, in Fabian Tract No. 41, Shaw says that in 1892 the Fabian delegates to the Vigilance Committee were, unlike those in 1885, instructed 'to use all their influence to avert a conflict with the police'.[9] Elsewhere he says that 'the Fabian does not intend to get thus handled if he can help it. If there is to be any shooting, he intends to be at the State end of the gun. And he knows that it will take him a good many years to get there.'[10] But Shaw does not seem to have been happy about this renunciation, and in an essay of 1889 he said that if they welcomed the necessity of a slow evolution to Socialism then they had been corrupted by their institutions 'to the most dastardly degree of selfishness'.[11] And in 1904 he said that violence would prob-

[5] Harris, pp. 135–6.
[6] John Parker and Donald Chapman, Preface, *Shaw and Society*, ed. C. E. M. Joad, 1953, p. 4.
[7] Harris, p. 98.
[8] Quoted by Alick West, *A Good Man Fallen Among Fabians*, 1950, p. 35.
[9] *Ibid.*, p. 36.
[10] Preface to 1908 reprint of *Fabian Essays*: quoted in *Shaw and Society*, ed. C. E. M. Joad, 1953, p. 94.
[11] *Fabian Essays* (1931 ed.), p. 186 f.; quoted by Alick West, *op. cit.*, p. 46.

ably still be necessary in the end but that it would take many years before the public could be educated to the necessity.[12]

As a polemical writer Shaw continued to be a socialist, even at times
a revolutionary socialist, until 1937, at which date he says in an
Author's Note to his *Intelligent Woman's Guide* (Pelican Edition) that
he is not just a Fabian pacifist, and, citing the Spanish War, says again
that revolution will be necessary. He claims that all he ever said was
that the transition to Socialism must be constructive and not destructive.[13] Other passages in the *Intelligent Woman's Guide* lend additional
testimony to his adherence to the socialist ideal.[14] He talks of the
superiority of Russian socialism to Western capitalism, maintaining that
it is even politically superior.[15] His frequent attacks on Democracy at
this period must not be construed as a loss of faith in Socialism but
rather as a loss of faith in Fabianism. An important deviation from
socialist doctrine occurs in *Everybody's Political What's What?*, published in 1944, where he defends piece-work and plays down the importance of equality of income, a mere 'mathematical abstraction'.[16]
He still emphasises equality of opportunity, however, and the deviation, although not ideologically unimportant, detracts but little from
Shaw's continued faith in Socialism. It may even be interpreted as a
mere doctrinaire divergence made for the sake of solidarity with
Russia, the bastion of Socialism.

But Shaw the artist was not Shaw the polemical writer, and Alick
West's Marxian diatribe against Shaw[17] is based mainly on an examination of his dramatic work. For, as Bentley points out, only in one of
Shaw's works of art, *An Unsocial Socialist*, his last novel (1883), does
he offer Socialism as a solution.[18] In this book Shaw comes nearest to
the world of vampire capitalists so beloved of many Marxists—
although not of Marx himself. Trefusis, the Socialist, sees stains of
blood and sweat on his wife's necklace,[19] and talks in highly coloured
moral terms of the wickedness of his capitalist grandfather and father,[20]
and even more strongly of the parasitic investors who helped to make
them wealthy.[21] But even at this early date Shavian realism rears its

---

[12] *The Clarion*, Oct. 21, 1904; quoted by Bentley, *Shaw*, pp. 36–7.
[13] *Intelligent Woman's Guide*, Author's Note.
[14] *Ibid.*, in particular Vol. II, pp. 350, 355–7, 363.   [15] *Ibid.*, Vol. II, p. 426.
[16] *Everybody's Political What's What?*, p. 57.
[17] *A Good Man Fallen Among Fabians*, 1950.   [18] Bentley, *Shaw*, p. 127.
[19] *An Unsocial Socialist*, Constable (standard edn.), 1950, p. 68.
[20] *Ibid.*, p. 73.   [21] *Ibid.*, p. 74.

head. The worker, as he was to become in Lickcheese in *Widowers'
Houses*, was also a capitalist in principle;[22] and of his father, Trefusis
says that he 'had to choose between being a slave himself and en-
slaving others. He chose the latter, and as he was applauded and made
much of for succeeding, who dare blame him? Not I.'[23] This is similar
to Mrs Warren's defence of her profession. This is the idea behind the
wit inversion that turned the tables, not only on Vivie Warren, but on
Trench in *Widowers' Houses*. For, although *Widowers' Houses* and
Mrs Warren's Profession belong to what we might call Shaw's first
period and are both whole-hearted attacks on the capitalist system, they
mark the beginning and the end of the absolutist approach inherent
in Marxian dogma. The relativism and pragmatism inherent in the
practice of wit began, after the comparatively humourless novels, to
assert itself. The class struggle might represent reality, but it was only
one aspect of reality and could not therefore provide a permanent
home for the vitalism of Shaw's wit. Only in a civic capacity can the
true artist be a party man.

But even in the plays it is Socialism as a panacea and a programme,
rather than the spirit of Socialism, that is abandoned. That by the time
of *John Bull's Other Island* (1904) and *Major Barbara* (1905) we find
exploitation conveying more benefits than Socialism, means that Shaw
despaired of the latter as an immediate and practical solution. In
Heartbreak House (1913–19), *The Apple Cart* (1929), and *On the Rocks*
(1933), he is still attacking capitalist ethos and tactics with vehemence
and bitterness. Of *On the Rocks* Edmund Wilson says: 'Then we rea-
lize that, after a detour of the better part of half a century, of almost the
whole of his artistic career, Shaw has only returned to that Bloody
Sunday of 1887 when the Socialists had headed a demonstration and
been driven away by the police.'[24]

Shaw did not despair of Socialism but of the integrity and ability
that would be necessary to put Socialism into practice. The witty
realist could not for long be comfortable in the same bed as Rousseau,
the emotional romantic, who with his doctrine of the natural goodness
of Man was perhaps the spiritual founder of modern Socialism.
Reality was compelled to admit the natural evil in Man and to place its
hopes not in doctrinaire idealism but in the man of will. It was this
more pragmatic ideal that coincided with the great period of Shavian

---

[22] *Ibid.*, p. 136.   [23] *Ibid.*, p. 204.
[24] Wilson, *Triple Thinkers*, pp. 185–6.

comedy, depending on the conflict between the witty realist and the bemused or brainsick romantic. *Arms and the Man* (1894), *Candida* (1894), *The Devil's Disciple* (1896), *Caesar and Cleopatra* (1898), *Captain Brassbound's Conversion* (1899), *Man and Superman* (1901–3), *John Bull's Other Island* (1904), *Major Barbara* (1905), are among the plays that belong to this period. In forsaking absolutist and socialist standards, the preacher became more closely integrated with the artist.

In the early plays of this period Shaw still retains the ebullient optimism often characteristic of the man of wit in the early stages of a literary career. His very exuberance in attack testifies to a continued faith in the teachability and the ability of Man to enter the lists and emerge triumphant. Pragmatism, too, wears a suit of shining armour; and, despite Shaw's repudiation of the moralist's position, moral laws are still partially valid, for we still know who is right and who is wrong. In these plays, however, the man of action bestows benefits which are only preached by ineffective doctrinaires.

But the propensity of wit to see all sides of the question is still with him. He may mock the romantic rebels like Brassbound, Sergius, Morell, Ramsden, Octavius, and Mendoza's gang of socialist hoboes; but what are the realists such as Anderson, Caesar, Bluntschli, Candida, Lady Cicely, Larry Doyle, Undershaft, Broadbent, and Cusins, but people who compromise with the devil? Can the man who is still a rebel socialist at heart make efficiency the only criterion? Is not a faith in the efficiency and benevolence of the man of action as naïve as a faith in socialist Utopias? Is it enough for the man of action to be benevolent and efficient if he is also stupid? And even if he is not stupid can he, working in the world as it is and with men as they are, make a significant contribution? The pragmatist and empiricist ultimately develop their own brand of determinism, one far more pessimistic than that of the absolutist.

As might be expected, then, the seeds of change are to be found in the great realist-romantic period no less than they were in the socialist period. A clear beginning of disillusion and despair is to be found in *John Bull's Other Island* (1904) and *Major Barbara* (1905), although there are strong symptoms in *Man and Superman* (1903) with its satire on arm-chair progress.[25] Shaw in his quest for reality finds a complex

[25] William Irvine in *The Universe of G.B.S.*, New York, 1949, says that the Anglo-Boer War was 'one of the most disillusioning events' of Shaw's life. See pp. 237, 293.

reality. In *John Bull's Other Island*, Broadbent, the realist, is not a vitalist but a rigid and sentimental idiot, who has need of an intelligent and spiritual amanuensis, Larry Doyle, to save his realism from lapsing into sham romanticism. Keegan, the 'romantic', has wit and a greater grasp of that inner reality which does not measure the world in terms of efficiency; and his 'madness' is clearly meant to be a mirror held up to an aspect of the truth of which Broadbent and even Doyle know nothing.

Superficially *Major Barbara* is more optimistic in temper. Man appears to compromise with his social environment and yet keep his soul intact. The play is an attempt to reconcile the saint and the realist. The eccentric Keegan has been transformed into an eminently practical saint in the person of Major Barbara, and the ludicrous Broadbent has been transformed into the witty Undershaft. But it is a spurious reconciliation, as Shaw seems to realise when he makes Cusins, the scholar, rather than Barbara, the saint, the chief object of the campaign of conversion. The very extreme to which Shaw went, by substituting a ruthless armaments manufacturer like Undershaft for a comparatively harmless entrepreneur like Broadbent, is perhaps a measure of his despairing determination to reconcile the irreconcilable. Undershaft's guilty repudiation of guilt in his motto of 'Unashamed'[26] might be applied to Shaw himself in this play. The man who fought vivisection so vehemently because he saw the necessity of a morality that is indivisible finds himself defending the manufacture of armaments out of which only an immediate advantage can be gained. And what was the immediate advantage? A regiment of workmen who had sold their souls not for the bread, margarine, and treacle of the Salvation Army shelter but for the bread, butter, and honey of a model township. Barbara is no more converted than Keegan or Shaw himself: there is only a temporary acquiescence. Only Cusins, the ironist, submits and, as Chesterton points out and Shaw unavailingly denies,[27] he puts up a poor fight.

There is, then, in *Major Barbara* no essential mitigation of Keegan's 'This world, sir, is very clearly a place of torment and penance, a place where the fool flourishes and the good and wise are hated and persecuted',[28] unless it is the wicked man rather than the fool who flourishes.

---

[26] *Major Barbara*, Act III, p. 497.
[27] 'Chesterton on Shaw', *Pen Portraits and Reviews*, Constable (standard edn.), 1949, p. 84.
[28] *John Bull's Other Island*, Act IV, p. 440.

'And this hypocrisy,' said Nietzsche, 'found I worst amongst them, that even those who command feign the virtues of those who serve.'[29] But Shaw was never really guilty of the hypocrisy of elevating Broadbent and Undershaft to the ranks of those who serve, for at this period he was not interested in motive. Indeed, it was probably partly the result of this abortive attempt to exclude moral considerations by one as morally earnest as Shaw that led him, in the years preceding and during the Great War, to lay less stress on the fundamental comic cleavage between romance and reality and to turn to themes which are, on the whole, of lesser political and social import. Production is prolific, but many of the plays are short and most of them are slight. It is for the most part a period of withdrawal, the growing frivolity masking a growing pessimism. There are few characters of any stature, for Man no longer controls his own destiny. In *Annajanska, the Bolshevik Empress* (1917), Revolution is nothing more than a shibboleth-ridden change of masters. In *The Inca of Perusalem* (1916), the man of steel is a man of straw. The major plays of the period are equally unconstructive and unsubstantial. The doctor's dilemma in the play (1906) is Shaw's dilemma, and remains unresolved simply because he cannot find it in himself to come down either on the side of successful action, as represented by the unscrupulous genius, Dubedat, or on the side of moral integrity, as represented by an unsuccessful but honest mediocrity, Blenkinsop. *Androcles and the Lion* (1912) is a significant play in recording Shaw's drift to despair. In returning to the theme of reconciliation between saintliness and reality, Shaw concludes with a rejection of both. Lavinia prepares herself for the lions without any conviction of salvation; and the only reconciliation takes place on a farcical level, with Androcles, a comic saint, making friends with reality in the form of a comic lion.

After the Indian summer of *Pygmalion* (1912), Shaw makes his return to the almost completely non-flippant treatment of a fundamental theme in *Heartbreak House*, begun in 1913 and finished in 1919. *Heartbreak House* is Shaw's *Troilus and Cressida*, and marks a complete collapse of his faith in a rational order of society. But the Great War, which consisted of 'innocent men killing one another. . . . For the devilment of the godless rulers of this world',[30] did more to Shaw than destroy his

[29] Friedrich Nietzsche, 'Thus Spake Zarathustra', tr. Thomas Common, *The Philosophy of Nietzsche*, Modern Library edn., New York, 1954, p. 187.
[30] *Too True to be Good*, Act III, p. 1162.

faith in Democracy, Fabianism, or any scheme of social amelioration. It destroyed his faith in Man. Both Man and Society are damned in *Heartbreak House*. It is, as Joad points out, one of the least didactic of Shaw's plays,[31] for he has lost faith not only in his previous teachings but in the educability of mankind. One could do little with Man as he was. Fabianism recognised the superable difficulties imposed by social heredity, but *Heartbreak House* goes much further by recognising the insuperable difficulties imposed by individual heredity. Reality can no longer exclude morality. The flight from Rousseau had finally plunged him into the bottomless pit of original sin. The play abandons utilitarian criteria and reeks of outraged morality. Money is no longer the liberating force as it was in *Major Barbara* and *John Bull's Other Island*, the snivelling pathos of Mangan, the deepest damned of all the characters, standing in strong contrast to the robust self-confidence of Broadbent and the Machiavellian geniality of Undershaft. The man of money and power has failed. Shotover, another eccentric, succeeds Keegan in the search for a means by which the truth can come into its own. But Shotover's senility merely emphasises the overwhelming sense of futility, which, at the end of the play, actually welcomes the bombers, deplores their departure, and looks forward to their return.

It was, then, with bitterness in his heart that Shaw returned to the task of reconstructing his political thinking. But successful reconstruction can seldom be achieved with salvaged materials. Remnants of his Socialism, of his admiration for the Man of Action, and of his period of disillusion were thrown together in a crazy ramshackle structure which at times seemed only fit for occupation by a clown. His first preoccupation in *Back to Methuselah* (1920) was the reconstruction of mankind itself. In *Man and Superman* (1903), written significantly enough, just before the first premature onset of despair in *John Bull's Other Island*, he had called for supermen, a race of philosopher-kings who would throw off the burden of social and individual heredity, who would not only see the good but also desire to follow it. In *Back to Methuselah*, he largely forsook the social for the biological. By a sustained effort of will Man must throw off the biological chains with which he has been loaded by Darwin and Freud. And because it required an effort of will, the new creed represented a reaction from the pessimism of *Heartbreak House*. Man was still free, set free by Bergson, Nietzsche, and Samuel Butler; for Shaw, although he often said that he was not a moralist,

[31] Joad, *Shaw*, p. 96.

joined with Samuel Butler in attacking Darwin for banishing not only mind but morality from the Universe.[32] Knowledge alone was not virtue; but Shaw could not, like Eliot, Waugh, Joad, and Toynbee seek a solution in revealed religion. His Creative Evolution was an intellectual and emotional rather than a teleological conception. With its dramatically useful but philosophically farcical 'long-livers', it was a compromise between pre-war rationalism and post-war anti-rationalism, a means of evading the eternal religious dilemma of choosing between a helpless God and an ominiscient God who was cruel or indifferent. Man could still feel that he was his own master, and, with the advent of the Superman, the equally eternal social question of *quis custodiet ipsos custodes* presumably also fell away.

Creative Evolution, however, was for Shaw partly an exercise in escape. It was a philosophical escape for one who could not subscribe to what he regarded as the inanities of revealed religion, but above all it was an escape from the present. And to one of Shaw's deeply rooted humanitarian habits of thought, it was not likely to be either a satisfying or a permanent escape. In *Saint Joan* (1923), he is back to his old theme of the reconciliation of the saint with the man of the here and now. But Saint Joan's concluding 'O God that madest this beautiful earth, when will it be ready to receive Thy saints? How long, O Lord, how long?[33] lacks Major Barbara's visionary, albeit rather determined, optimism, and sets the spiritual stage for the plays that follow. Athenian Democracy killed Socrates and turned Plato's thoughts to his oligarchic Republic as the only framework in which the philosopher-king could exert power. In the Epilogue to *Saint Joan*, twentieth-century Democracy rejected Saint Joan. So much the worse for Democracy is the theme that dominates the political extravaganzas and allegories that make up a great part of the dramatic production of Shaw's last period.

But it must not be thought that Shaw's espousal of fascist methods was a marriage of the heart. Many idealisms start in the name of individual freedom and end in authoritarianism, for the idealists become authoritarian in order to promote and perpetuate their ideal and in order to force others to conform. Christianity gave rise to the authoritariansim of the Catholic Church, the Reformation to the various forms of Protestant authoritarianism, Rousseauism to Jacobinism, Socialism to the dictatorship of Stalin More pragmatic creeds such as Shaw's are not exempt from this Nemesis. Bertrand Russell sees authoritarian

[32] *Sixteen Self Sketches*, No. XIII, pp. 75-6.   [33] *Saint Joan*, Epilogue, p. 1009.

implications in the pragmatism of even such a good democrat as Dewey. Shaw did not like Fascism, but he thought that it was better than Liberalism because it trained the citizen to take a corporate view of the State.[34] What had Liberalism done for the people except cry liberty? And said Shaw: 'Those who cry Liberty when there is no liberty are as unbearable as those who cry Peace when there is no Peace.'[35] Fascism at least faced reality and got things done. 'I am not so much concerned about their freedom as Mr Chesterton; for it is plain to me that our civilization is being destroyed by the monstrously excessive freedom we allow to individuals.'[36] But Shaw knew that Fascism was essentially capitalist. 'Fascism,' he said, 'breaks down, not on liberty and democracy, neither of which have any real existence under developed Capitalism, but on distribution; and if Fascism remedies that, it becomes Communism.[37] In other words, Shaw did little more than voice, with his customary over-emphasis, the range of millions who found that political democracy gave them the vote instead of a good dinner. He might proclaim a Superman or a Nietzschean morality with its shift from the social to the individual. In his wrath against the verbal gyrations of the Stanley Baldwins and Ramsay MacDonalds and against the apostasy of the Labour Party of the 'twenties and 'thirties, he might launch into extravagant praise of Mussolini or into dogged defences of totalitarian liquidations in Russia and elsewhere, but his essential adherence to humanist values remained unchanged. *The Apple Cart* (1929), *Too True To Be Good* (1931), *The Simpleton of the Unexpected Isles* (1934), and particularly *On the Rocks* (1933) with its despair of cerebral man and yearnings for the Man on Horseback, are still shot through with compassion and fellow-feeling for the ordinary man, whose chronic credulity and incapacity he so much deplored. These plays are also shot through with the bitterness of a man who had spent his life trying to build a palace out of driftwood.

Enough has been said in this very brief summary of Shaw's political and philosophical pilgrimage to show that his thought, although not inconsistent, is not uniform or changeless. Edmund Wilson in *Triple Thinkers*, which contains one of the best analyses of Shaw as a thinker, says:

[34] *Intelligent Woman's Guide*, Vol. II, p. 454.   [35] *Ibid.*, Vol. II, p. 454.
[36] 'Chesterton on Eugenics', *Pen Portraits and Reviews*, Constable (standard edn.), 1949, p. 102.
[37] *Intelligent Woman's Guide*, Author's Note.

The real Shaw has thus never been the single-minded crusader that people at one time used to think him. Except for a limited period during the eighties and early nineties—when he wrote his only straight socialist plays, *Widowers' Houses* and *Mrs Warren's Profession* —he has never really been a practising socialist. And I am inclined to believe that the future will exactly reverse the opinion which his contemporaries have usually had of him. It used always to be said of Shaw that he was primarily not an artist, but a promulgator of certain ideas. The truth is, I think, that he is a considerable artist, but that his ideas—that is, his social philosophy proper—have always been confused and uncertain.[38]

And it is with Shaw, the artist, a very long-lived artist, that this study is concerned. The contrast between the credulous over-confidence of youth and the cautious expediency of querulous old age has been noted by writers since the time of Aristotle. The form and expression given to these characteristics will vary according to the traditions and stage of development reached in any particular civilization; and Shaw's progression through radicalism, the cult of the individual, the contempt of the masses, and a religious or higher synthesis is no more 'confused and uncertain' than that of many of his contemporaries. It is typical of many intellectuals who, divorced from traditional norms, fall prey to inner conflicts which can only be resolved by changing or advocating changes in society. It is even more typical of the intellectual who is also an artist; for he is usually more aware of these inner conflicts, more aware of self. A glance at Shaw's self is also necessary to understand the evolution of his wit and satire.

2. CHARACTER

Most writers on Shaw are agreed upon his isolation from his fellowmen. Of himself there is the much quoted 'Whether it be that I was born mad or a little too sane, my kingdom was not of this world: I was at home only in the realm of my imagination, and at my ease only with the mighty dead'.[39] Hugh Kingsmill comments on his rootlessness and indifference to individuals;[40] Maurice Colbourne deplores his 'lack of common touch with humanity' which lays 'a great sterility

[38] Wilson, *Triple Thinkers*, p. 163.   [39] *Immaturity*, Prefaces, p. 648.
[40] Hugh Kingsmill, *The Progress of a Biographer*, 1949, p. 51.

upon his work';[41] Chesterton says of him that 'He did not start from home, but from homelessness'[42] and that he has never had Piety, Roman Pietas;[43] Joad notes his 'embarrassingly impersonal' demeanour[44] and his monopolistic conversation,[45] which is certainly not inconsistent with what his secretary, Blanche Patch, says of him as a taciturn and disappointing guest.[46] Bentley speaks of the isolation from youth of one who 'is farther apart from his contemporaries than any thinker since Nietzsche', one who was 'born and bred a Protestant in the most fanatically Catholic city in the world . . . Practically the only thing his education taught him was how to stand alone. His keenest pleasures were those which the imagination could feast on without intrusion from people around him. . . . The first time he felt the pressure of society was when he became a clerk. It was too much for him. He broke with his whole environment by going to seek his fortune in London. . . . Mother and son continued to see little of each other. Shaw entered British society by the Bohemian gate. He never tried to become an established member of the upper, middle, or lower class. He remained "unassimilated" . . . in the twentieth century [he] has barely pretended to be a part of our world at all. At best he descends upon us from his country house at Ayot St. Lawrence like a prophet descending from mountain solitude.'[47]

Brought up, then, in a needy home presided over by a drunken father and a withdrawn mother, Shaw spent his youth lost in loneliness, intense shyness, and magniloquent day-dreams. He himself said that he was like Charles Matthews in the farce *Cool as a Cucumber*, the tale of a conversion from extreme bashfulness to outrageous impudence.[48] But Shaw never got over his childhood; and the process of coming to terms with society, like that attempted by a host of artists, was always partial and always subject to frequent reversals. The first attempt was made by means of Socialism. A less satisfactory means, however, it would be hard to find.

For the intellectual of the nineteenth and twentieth centuries Socialism was primarily not an economic but a spiritual revolt. It was a new revelation, with Marx as its prophet, for those who had rejected reve-

[41] Maurice Colbourne, *The Real Bernard Shaw*, 1949, p. 150.
[42] Chesterton, p. 267.   [43] *Ibid.*, p. 269.   [44] Joad, *Shaw*, p. 33.
[45] *Ibid.*, p. 35.   [46] Blanche Patch, *Thirty Years with G.B.S.*, 1951, p. 244.
[47] Bentley, *Shaw*, pp. 215–17.
[48] *Immaturity*, Prefaces, p. 648; quoted by Bentley, *Shaw*, p. 218.

lation. It was an attempt to fashion a society in which career would be open to talent, and in which talent would be free to develop and express itself untrammelled by a competitive and philistine capitalism. But being a revolt, it was scarcely a means for coming to terms with society. Shaw himself knew that the intellectual vanguard of Socialism was composed of people of an individualistic rather than a collectivist turn of mind. Writing of Belloc he says: 'Belloc, like most anti-Socialists, is intensely gregarious. He cannot bear isolation or final ethical responsibility: he clings to the Roman Catholic Church: he clung to his French nationality because one nation was not enough for him: he went into the French Army because it gave him a regiment, a company, even a gun to cling to: he was not happy until he got into Parliament; and now his one dread is that he will not get into heaven.'[49] Moreover, in the condemnation of others there is usually approbation of self; and Shaw is here elevating his own isolation into a virtue, particularly as it is linked with the idea of 'ethical responsibility'. 'Finding one's place may be made very puzzling', he writes, 'by the fact that there is no place in ordinary society for extraordinary individuals.'[50] But the loneliness of genius is accentuated by the introversion which accompanies genius, and one of the marks of introversion is often an emphasis on moral principles. The introvert sees his hermit retreat as a moral ivory tower. He preaches equality and eschews fraternity because the one is abstract and the other requires a social adjustment of which he is not capable. As a means of extroversion, then, Shaw's Socialism was a failure. Not merely from an ideological but also from a psychological standpoint, a new departure was necessary, a departure that would take him away from the isolated heroes and heroines of *Cashel Byron's Profession*, *An Unsocial Socialist*, and *Immaturity*, away from the priggish self-immolation of Vivie Warren of *Mrs Warren's Profession* to the men of action, to the masters of reality who threw themselves into the world as it is. This new attempt at extroversion coincided more or less with Shaw's fully-fledged entry into the field of comedy.

It also gave rise to fresh inner conflict, constituting as it did a violation of Shaw's innermost convictions, of which it was found necessary to say something in writing of his political development. There is little

[49] 'The Chesterbelloc', *Pen Portraits and Reviews*, Constable (standard edn.), 1949, p. 75.
[50] Quoted by Wilson, *Triple Thinkers*, p. 160.

more to add. When extroversion through men of action had taken him to such extremes as to make heroes of an extroverted idiot like Broadbent and to an 'unashamed', rapacious, and essentially amoral armaments manufacturer like Undershaft, a partial relapse into introversion and despair took place. The pessimism which is nearly always implicit in introversion joined forces with the pessimism inherent in pragmatism.

To the next period, too, there is little need to add to what has already been said. He sought to come to terms with Society, not through the portrayal of men of action, but in increased frivolity. If the world will not listen to him, it will at least laugh with him. But, as Lucas says, 'We have seen, again and again, how the neurotic is like a caterpillar, whose tail is fastened to a point behind him, while Time drags his head forward and forward; till the tension and the strain end in a split'.[51] The term 'neurotic', unless carefully defined in context, is almost meaningless. Anybody who is not fool or rogue enough to think that complete conformity is the panacea for personal problems can be described as a neurotic, and the term is applied to Shaw without derogatory intent. Shaw's tail, like all our tails, was tied to his own childhood and the 'split'—or perhaps 'recoil' would be the better word—came with the Great War and *Heartbreak House*. Shotover-Shaw was alone again, kicking despairingly at the debris of his own personal Heartbreak House.

Even in 1883 when Shaw was at his most maladjusted, Trefusis, the most Unsocial Socialist of them all, had said 'wishes for the destruction of the human race, however rational and sincere, are contrary to nature', and added 'what a precious fool I should be if I were working at an international association of creatures only fit for destruction!'[52] But the Shaw of 1919 no longer believed in the possibility of such an association. He was back in himself again. The bombers could come for all he cared. Nor could he have replied 'It seems so' as Ellie did to Shotover when he asked if she was 'one of those who are so sufficient to themselves that they are only happy when they are stripped of everything, even of hope?'[53] No matter in what intellectual *culs-de-sac* Shaw might find himself, he was never overcome by paralysis of the will, by emotional anaesthesia. In his attempt at extroversion by identifying

[51] F. L. Lucas, *Literature and Psychology*, 1951, p. 250.
[52] *An Unsocial Socialist* (1883), Constable (standard edn.), 1950, p. 96.
[53] *Heartbreak House*, Act II, p. 791.

himself with the man of action, he had abandoned the intellectual position of socialist rationalism by an act of faith, by an affirmation of faith in life for its own sake. The affirmation is now renewed by resuscitating the creed of Creative Evolution. A belief in action for its own sake had been a far too extravagant violation of his own nature. Something with a more positive philosophical and intellectual attestation must be sought. Which is almost to say that extroversion must compromise with introversion.

Jung, who crystallised the thinking of a hundred *littérateurs*, saw in the over-intellectualisation of urbanised man the chief source of modern neurosis. Mental equilibrium can only be achieved by maintaining a balance between the conscious and unconscious, and with the decline in the traditional standards the emphasis is too much on the conscious. Religion in particular provides the ready-made set of values and beliefs necessary to give the individual a sense of community, continuity, and ultimate meaning. If religion breaks down then the individual either turns in on himself or seeks unconventional outlets. Creative Evolution partook of both 'solutions'. It was an essay in extroversion in so far as it provided a faith, a means of escaping from a suffering present to a more hopeful future, and a share in the shaping of one's own destiny. But it was an essay in introversion in so far as it substituted a God within for an external God, and diverted man's aspirations to a future that was fantastic by virtue of its very remoteness. For a Nietzsche such a creed became a crazy retreat into a dream world in which he himself became God. For a Shaw the only danger was a lapse into insincerity. Said Joad: '. . . an incommunicable order of reality, his resources break down when he seeks in his plays to convey its nature. For he entertains its existence, in so far as he does entertain it, as a supposition of the intellect and not as a need of the spirit; it is a concession to fairmindedness by the head rather than the satisfaction of a demand by the heart.'[54] Joad was wrong in saying that it was not a need of the spirit with Shaw, but he was right in saying that 'Mystical talk in the mouths of Shaw's characters is a mere bombination of words, simply because he does not in his heart believe in the existence of any supernatural order to which the words could relate.'[55] For Shaw retained what a Chesterton might call his insane sanity to the end.

Wrong, too, was Benn Levy when he said of Shaw that he 'was a comedian as he was a creative evolutionist, because he was an opti-

[54] Joad, *Shaw*, pp. 50–1.   [55] *Ibid.*, p. 49.

mist.'[56] Neither the comic spirit nor the seeking of sanctuary in religious or philosophical systems are symptoms of optimism. After seeking brief sanctuary in the year A.D. 31920 or *As Far As Thought Can Reach*, which is the title of Part V of *Back to Methuselah*, came the remarkable *tour de force* of *Saint Joan*. But *Saint Joan* showed that he could not find it in himself to attempt any new orientation or adjustment. Consequently for the rest of his life, beyond dabbling in totalitarian makeshifts which were bolt-holes rather than solutions, Shaw had nothing new to say. It was merely a question of how he was going to say it.

[56] Benn W. Levy, 'Shaw the Dramatist', *Shaw and Society*, ed. C. E. M. Joad, 1953, p. 273.

CHAPTER VI

The Nemesis of Wit

IT NOW remains to investigate the interaction of Shaw's spiritual and ideological development with his wit and satire, the technique by which he sought to express himself and to impose his ideas on the world.

Perhaps there is nothing more hostile to the practice of wit than the single-minded adoption of a cause. The fanatic with his *idée fixe*, the specialist with his speciality, the preacher with his simplification, are notorious for their lack of humour. In the Socialist period, which began with the early novels and 'ended' with *Mrs Warren's Profession*, Shaw was a preacher, and his wit was only in its adolescent stage. Very much the moralist, his main attack was on vice rather than on folly. Of course, as the exposure of Trench's unconscious culpability in *Widowers' Houses* and Vivie Warren's unjustified condemnation of her mother in *Mrs Warren's Profession* show, Shaw was well aware that vice and folly are not always separable and are equally productive of evil; but nevertheless even in these plays the appeal, as always when vice is stressed, is to the feelings more than to the intellect, particularly in *Mrs Warren's Profession*, where Crofts is perhaps the only completely loathsome character in Shaw.

Moreover, the vice attacked is almost exclusively capitalist vice. However much Shaw might consciously guard against the imputation, these early works smack of neo-Marxian melodrama and the tone is one of outraged morality with the workers as the victims. His wit, with its more intellectual penetration into the distinction between romance and reality, with the emphasis on folly instead of vice, was not yet fully developed. As it did develop, a more pragmatic, a more relativist standpoint was an inevitable outcome. If culpability there was, the worker was equally culpable, as the financial elevation of Lick-cheese in *Widower's Houses* foreshadowed. Galsworthy, whose early career was also marked by an effort to achieve detachment, said: 'We find ourselves so near that thing which has no breadth, the middle line, that we can watch them both, and positively smile to see the fun.'[1] Shaw, too, tried to take up his position on the middle line and managed to smile to see the fun until *Heartbreak House*, when vice and folly became as one. He was, however, less successful than Galsworthy, for his desertion of revolutionary socialism and his whole-hearted adoption of wit as his vehicle were both needs of the spirit rather than an attempt to achieve artistic detachment. His isolation put him in a position to achieve the detachment necessary for the practice of wit, and was at the same time a spur to extroversion. As already remarked, all art is an attempt at extroversion and a resolution of inner conflict: 'it does so, like any other activity, by changing the environment to express the repressed needs'.[2] But wit, in particular, is directed outwards. 'This intelligence, however, must always remain in touch with other intelligences. .... You would hardly appreciate the comic if you felt yourself isolated from others. Laughter appears to stand in need of an echo.'[3] Add to this Freud's statement that 'the subjective conditions of wit are so frequently fulfilled in the case of neurotic persons',[4] and there seems little doubt that wit is the outcome of a feeling of defeat. Shaw sought consolation for his failure to extrovert himself through Socialism, not merely by attacking a society to which he had no feeling of belonging, but by rising superior to it; and there is probably no better way of achieving such a superiority than through amused contemplation of romantic illusions and enthusiasms.

But, as has been pointed out by many writers, the impulse to satirise anything usually implies that it exerts a strong, if unwelcome, attraction for the satirist. Baffled idealism or romanticism is the obverse side of the quest for reality. On his own confession, Shaw's youth had been spent amidst romantic daydreams. The very extravagance with which he embraced reality as embodied in the man of action contains more than an element of romanticism. He protested too much.

Moreover, extroversion through an emphasis on action, that most common means of extroversion, is with Shaw incomplete. Dick Dudgeon, who turns out to be a romantic, remains the real hero of *The Devil's Disciple*; and a halo of romance surrounds the heads of

---

[1] Preface to revised edition, *The Island Pharisees;* quoted by R. A. Scott-James, *Fifty Years of English Literature*, 1956, pp. 43–4.

[2] Paul Goodman, *The Structure of Literature*, Chicago, 1954, p. 11.

[3] Bergson, p. 5.   [4] Freud, p. 285.

such realists as Caesar, Bluntschli, Undershaft, and Tanner, a halo which
shines no less brightly round the head of Magnus in 1930. It was only in
the periods of despair that the man of action ceased to be romantic.
For the most part, too, Shaw's men of action still reflect his isolation.
They are very much in the world but are not part of it. They are in
fact supermen, and in their lack of love as well as hate they resemble
the lonely heroes and heroines of the early novels and *Mrs Warren's
Profession*. It is their wit that makes them different from these early
Shavians. Which is almost another way of saying that they are no
longer burdened with the hypertrophic conscience by which so many
introverts are possessed.

Horace Walpole's dictum that this world is a comedy to those that
think and a tragedy to those that feel is, in various guises, a commonplace of literary criticism. The process of extroversion through wit
is an attempt to substitute thinking for feeling. To Bergson the comic
is possible only when it is accompanied by something like an 'anesthe-
sia of the heart'.[5] To Freud, 'the comic feeling comes most in tolerably
indifferent cases which evince no strong feelings or interests'.[6] To
Arland Ussher, 'Comedy, in the best sense, is a symbolisation of the
life of the mind, the life "beyond good and evil" '.[7] To Worcester, 'the
time spent by the author in aiming his shaft gave him a chance to let
his emotions cool and to approach his subject through reason'.[8] The
so-called Shaw heartlessness has already been mentioned as a wit
technique. But it was more than a technique. Says Nietzsche: 'He
who cannot find the way to *his* ideal, lives more frivolously and shame-
lessly than the man without an ideal.'[9] In other words wit was a self-
protective device, a cloak for what Bertrand Russell's first wife called
Shaw's 'burning sympathy for the underdog'.[10] So far did he go in this
wit inversion of socialist romanticism that the revolutionaries and
workers of this post-socialist era nearly all became ridiculous, pathetic,
or despicable. In *Candida*, Morell, the strong-willed socialist, finally
stands revealed as a sermonising weakling. Gunner, the socialist clerk
in *Misalliance*, is a snivelling, blustering nincompoop. The dirty, in-
gratiating Drinkwater in *Captain Brassbound's Conversion*, the revolu-

[5] Bergson, p. 5.   [6] Freud, p. 357.
[7] Arland Ussher, *Three Great Irishmen*, 1952, p. 60.   [8] Worcester, p. 48.
[9] Friedrich Nietzsche, 'Beyond Good and Evil', tr. Helen Zimmern, *The Philosophy of Nietzsche*, Modern Library edn., New York, 1954, p. 463.
[10] Quoted by Blanche Patch, *Thirty Years with G.B.S.*, 1951, p. 175.

tionary tramps of the Sierra Nevada in *Man and Superman*, the Irish peasants in *John Bull's Other Island*, the derelicts of the Salvation Army shelter and the workers in Undershaft's armament factory in *Major Barbara* are nearly all held up to derision, almost to obloquy. There is, of course, an explicit or implicit understanding of the conditions which produce these pitiful types, but the concentration on desirable ends at the expense of morally motivated means finally produced an effect which was the reverse of what Shaw really intended. 'Hiroshima and Nagasaki are already rebuilt; and Japan is all the better for the change.'[11]

For Wit, like nearly all apparently successful techniques of adjustment, has its nemesis. If, as the Old Testament says, 'the end of mirth is heaviness', the end of satire is bitterness. The melancholic clown is such a famous typological paradox, exemplified in the lives of so many purveyors of humour, that only cause and not effect need be discussed. The cause lies in the very nature of wit, which is condemned to ultimate sterility because by attacking what Bergson calls 'system' it cannot itself be the means of erecting a system. It is true that it must have norms to provide a basis for attack, but these norms in their turn develop into a system equally vulnerable to attack. A chain reaction is set up in which causality becomes merely an arbitrarily and subjectively selected arrangement of events, in which the chicken and the egg take precedence over each other according to the exigencies of the moment. Wit always sees the cause behind the cause. It bites the hand that feeds it and finally turns on itself. For Truth, of which Wit is the errant handmaid, finally discovers that the only thing that gives Life a meaning is the search for a meaning.

Such a relativist standpoint was what Hegel regarded as a kind of cosmic impiety, and was what A. W. Schegel found in the irony which is implicit in so much literature, including Shakespeare.[12] I. A. Richards and T. S. Eliot seem to be assuming that irony and wit are finite in their operations by suggesting that their function is to reconcile discordant elements. Said Richards: 'The equilibrium of opposed impulses, which we suspect to be the ground-plan of the most valuable aesthetic responses, brings into play far more of our personality than is possible in experiences of a more defined emotion. We cease to be orientated in one definite direction . . . A state of mind which is not disinterested is

---

[11] *Buoyant Billions*, Act I, p. 1371. Spoken by The Son, the 'world betterer'.

[12] A. W. Schlegel, *Lectures on Dramatic Art and Literature*, Lecture XXIII, 1809–11, tr. John Black, 1815.

one which sees things only from one standpoint or under one aspect.'[13]

Certainly Shaw achieved not the 'equilibrium' which Richards said should ideally be the product of irony, but 'irresolution'. In his early years, he said in *Maxims for Revolutionists*, 'The golden rule is that there are no golden rules'.[14] At the end of his life he said that he stood for Nothing.[15] And it was the exercise of wit, with its pragmatic basis, that contributed so much to the feeling of frustration which found political expression in authoritarianism, often the last refuge of the pragmatist, and philosophical expression in the remote Utopianism of Creative Evolution.

The stepping down to an almost flippant reality, which has already been noted at the end of Shaw's plays, is almost a confession that the wit technique can achieve nothing beyond a mere analysis. It has been said of Shaw that he 'was marvellous over a short distance; but he could not sustain an argument for more than a paragraph. This is why plays suited him so well. A second character could always interrupt when the first ran dry. There is no development; only statement and counter-statement.'[16] It is doubtful if anybody who was taking the whole body of Shaw's polemical work into account would have made such a criticism, which is, however, useful as a comment on the shortcomings of wit as a method and a way of thinking.

And failure to find a goal that was both true and good contributed greatly to the feeling of despair which had such a profound effect on Shaw's writing. The ideal—in the non-Ibsenite sense—failed to survive the continual intrusions of the witty or ironic real.

[13] I. A. Richards, *Principles of Literary Criticism*, 1924, p. 251.
[14] *Man and Superman*, Prefaces, p. 188.
[15] A. J. P. Taylor, *The Observer*, July 22, 1956, p. 6, col. 5.
[16] *Ibid.*, p. 6, col. 3.

CHAPTER VII

Wit as Evasion

IT IS now time to revert to the closing remarks of the chapter on irony, in which the different attitudes of the philosopher and the ironist to a breakdown of constructive effort were discussed. Brief mention has already been made of the attempts of Shaw, the philosopher, to overcome despair through a higher synthesis; and it now remains to examine the effects of ironic acceptance and flippant avoidance on Shaw's wit and satire.

I. TRAGEDY

Ironic acceptance springs from a realisation of the powerlessness of humanity to control its own destiny. It will, in seeking expression, be closely allied to tragedy; for tragedy is a revelation of the greatest joke of all, with all mankind reduced to a state of puppetry. Nothing burlesques so well as tragedy; for just as comedy is close to tears when it mingles with pathos, so is tragedy close to laughter if the pathos is excluded and stark inevitability alone remains. It is laughter in its most elemental form, laughter at the discomfiture of another, laughter which springs from grim satisfaction that nobody, not even the most exalted, is exempt from the cruel working of time and fate. For in tragedy, inevitability is almost completely divorced from the unexpected; and whenever the factor of time intrudes itself as a dominant, uncontrollable, but not unpredictable factor, the work of art will usually be tragic in tone. Not that tragedy is necessarily the product of despair. The classic, cathartic, conception of tragedy implies ultimate hope and harmony. But there is no hope and no harmony when there is no catharsis, or when catharsis is attempted by a sudden reversion from ultimate implications to the more comfortable reassurances of comedy and its preoccupation with a more malleable, or potentially more malleable, present.

Such was the use to which Shaw put comedy during his first and, as far as overt expression is concerned, very brief period of despair. In *John Bull's Other Island*, Larry Doyle's answer to Keegan's concern with man as a moral being living under the aspect of eternity crystallizes the playwright's rejection of the tragic approach:

> LARRY. In either case it would be an impertinence, Mr Keegan, as your approval is not of the slightest consequence to us. What use do you suppose all this drivel is to men with serious practical business in hand?
>
> *John Bull's Other Island*, Act IV, p. 451.

This is more than what Stephen Potter calls Shaw's 'nervous revulsion from the undiluted seriousness of the tragic moment',[1] so conspicuous in *The Doctor's Dilemma*. It is a rejection of the ethos of tragedy, with its sense of sin, in favour of that of comedy. But it cannot alter the tone of the play which, if it remains a comedy in space, is a tragedy in time.

In *Major Barbara*, too, there is an evasion of the ultimately tragic consequences of the destruction of Cusins's humanism and Barbara's Christian ethic by an emphasis on the present:

> CUSINS (*overjoyed*). Then you—you—you——Oh for my drum! (*He flourishes imaginary drumsticks.*)
>
> BARBARA (*angered by his levity*). Take care, Dolly, take care. Oh, if only I could get away from you and from father and from it all! if I could have the wings of a dove and fly away to heaven!
>
> CUSINS. And leave me!
>
> BARBARA. Yes, you, and all the other naughty mischievous children of men. But I cant. I was happy in the Salvation Army for a moment. I escaped from the world into a paradise of enthusiasm and prayer and soul saving; but the moment our money ran short, it all came back to Bodger: it was he who saved our people: he, and the Prince of Darkness, my papa. Undershaft and Bodger: their hands stretch everywhere: when we feed a starving fellow creature, it is with their bread, because there is no other bread; when we tend the sick, it is in the hospitals they endow; if we turn from the churches they build, we must kneel on the stones of the streets they

[1] Potter, p. 33.

pave. As long as that lasts, there is no getting away from them. Turning our backs on Bodger and Undershaft is turning our backs on life.

Major Barbara, Act III, p. 502.

But Shaw, in refusing to turn his back on life in the present, was turning his back on life in the future. The tragedy of Barbara's broken heart was not averted by any genuine reconciliation between her aspirations and her immediate fate. Barbara may be angered by Cusins's levity and his flourishing of drumsticks, but it was an ironically mischievous assault on the drums that marked the beginning of his conversion to Undershaftism:

> CUSINS. It is a wedding chorus from one of Donizetti's operas; but we have converted it. We convert everything to good here, including Bodger. You remember the chorus. 'For thee immense rejoicing—immenso giubilo—immenso giubilo.' (*With drum obbligato.*) Rum tum ti tum tum, tum tum ti ta——
>
> BARBARA. Dolly: you are breaking my heart.
>
> CUSINS. What is a broken heart more or less here? Dionysos Undershaft has descended. I am possessed.

Ibid., Act II, p. 485.

Comedy is used as a means of avoiding the fundamental conflict between the present and the eternal.)

In *Heartbreak House*, however, the suppressions and evasions of *Major Barbara* and *John Bull's Other Island* are no longer in evidence. The tragic sense of time with its complement, the sense of sin, dominate the play. Undershaft, the benevolent superman, has become 'Mangan and his mutual admiration gang'. Broadbent, the benevolent fool, has become a force for evil. Action in the present is futile:

> HECTOR. But I have children. All that is over and done with for me: and yet I too feel that this cant last. We sit here talking, and leave everything to Mangan and to chance and to the devil. Think of the powers of destruction that Mangan and his mutual admiration gang wield! It's madness: it's like giving a torpedo to a badly brought up child to play at earthquakes with.
>
> MAZZINI. I know. I used often to think about that when I was young.
>
> HECTOR. Think! Whats the good of thinking about it? Why didnt you do something?

MAZZINI. But I did. I joined societies and made speeches and wrote pamphlets. That was all I could do. But, you know, though the people in the societies thought they knew more than Mangan, most of them wouldnt have joined if they had known as much. You see they had never had any money to handle or any men to manage. Every year I expected a revolution, or some frightful smash-up: it seemed impossible that we could blunder and muddle on any longer. But nothing happened, except, of course, the usual poverty and crime and drink that we are used to. Nothing ever does happen. It's amazing how well we get along, all things considered.

LADY UTTERWORD. Perhaps somebody cleverer than you and Mr Mangan was at work all the time.

MAZZINI. Perhaps so. Though I was brought up not to believe in anything, I often feel that there is a great deal to be said for the theory of an over-ruling Providence, after all.

Heartbreak House, Act III, p. 800.

In *Heartbreak House* no catharsis through comedy is attempted. The wit is not the wit of attack but of ironic withdrawal, the wit that exposes for the sake of exposure and not for the sake of conversion:

ELLIE. There seems to be nothing real in the world except my father and Shakespear. Marcus's tigers are false; Mr Mangan's millions are false; there is nothing really strong and true about Hesione but her beautiful black hair; and Lady Utterword's is too pretty to be real. The one thing that was left to me was the Captain's seventh degree of concentration; and that turns out to be——

CAPTAIN SHOTOVER. Rum.

LADY UTTERWORD (*placidly*). A good deal of my hair is quite genuine. The Duchess of Dithering offered me fifty guineas for this (*touching her forehead*) under the impression that it was a transformation; but it is all natural except the color.

MANGAN (*wildly*). Look here: I'm going to take off all my clothes (*he begins tearing off his coat*).

LADY UTTERWORD		Mr Mangan!
CAPTAIN SHOTOVER	(*in consternation*).	Whats that?
HECTOR		Ha! ha! Do. Do.
ELLIE		Please dont.

MRS HUSHABYE (*catching his arm and stopping him*). Alfred: for shame! Are you mad?

MANGAN. Shame! What shame is there in this house? Let's all strip stark naked. We may as well do the thing thoroughly when we're about it. Weve stripped ourselves morally naked: well, let us strip ourselves physically naked as well, and see how we like it. I tell you I cant bear this. I was brought up to be respectable. I dont mind the women dyeing their hair and the men drinking: it's human nature. But it's not human nature to tell everybody about it. Every time one of you opens your mouth I go like this (*he cowers as if to avoid a missile*) afraid of what will come next. How are we to have any self-respect if we dont keep it up that we're better than we really are?

LADY UTTERWORD. I quite sympathize with you, Mr Mangan. I have been through it all; and I know by experience that men and women are delicate plants and must be cultivated under glass. Our family habit of throwing stones in all directions and letting the air in is not only unbearably rude, but positively dangerous. Still, there is no use catching physical colds as well as moral ones; so please keep your clothes on.

Ibid., Act III, p. 797.

Saint Joan is Shaw's one attempt at tragedy in the classic sense and, together with *Back to Methuselah*, marks an attempt at reconstruction. Joan dies reconciled:

JOAN. . . . . I know that your counsel is of the devil, and that mine is of God.

. . . . . .

LADVENU. You wicked girl: if your counsel were of God would He not deliver you?

JOAN. His ways are not your ways. He wills that I go through the fire to His bosom; for I am His child, and you are not fit that I should live among you. That is my last word to you.

Saint Joan, Sc. VI, p. 1000.

Arland Ussher says that Saint Joan 'is not perhaps (like Ibsen's *Ghosts*) a true tragedy, but it is a highly fascinating drama of ideas; for Shaw's admirable knack of "seeing both sides"—never shown to better advantage than in the Trial Scene—is in fact the comedic genius and not the tragic one'.[2] But although Shaw sees both sides, there is a definite emotional and not intellectual identification with the one side. It is only in the Epilogue that there is an attempt to replace a tragic by a comedic catharsis.

2. HUMOUR

The wit of ironic withdrawal may almost be equated with humour. Any analysis of the nature of wit in this study has been adventitious and not systematic, and there is no intention of adding to the numerous attempts to distinguish between wit and humour, attempts which have no more chance of succeeding than attempts to separate the elements in a chemical compound by mechanical means. It can be said that wit presupposes a confident norm but humour does not. Yet, as has been noted, the norm for wit is a shifting norm. It can be said that humour is based on sympathy and acquiescence but wit is not. Yet, as the shifting norm indicates, wit sees both sides of the question. It can be said that humour is based on self-analysis but wit is not. Yet all art is ultimately based on self-analysis, and wit is subjective in origin and development. It can be said that wit is attacking and proselytizing but humour is not. Yet the distinction is perhaps not valid except in so far as wit necessarily attacks orthodoxy with more vehemence than humour attacks unorthodoxy. It can be said that humour is compassionate but wit is not. Yet, by its very vehemence, wit betrays a perhaps deeper, although less direct, compassion than humour. How difficult it is to separate wit from humour may be judged from two conflicting views of Shaw. Chesterton says that Shaw 'has no nonsensical second self . . . his wit is never a weakness; therefore it is never a sense of humour. For wit is always connected with the idea that truth is close and clear. Humour, on the other hand, is always connected with the idea that truth is tricky and mystical and easily mistaken.'[3] Stephen Potter says: 'In the half dozen great plays, we see a different kind of humour altogether. In these, humour comes near to compassion.'[4] And of *Candida* he goes on to say that 'The play is full of humour—but in the case even of the comedy types, like Prossy the love-crossed, the humour is tinged with sympathy and comprehension'.[5]

---

[2] Arland Ussher, *Three Great Irishmen*, 1952, p. 35.
[3] Chesterton, pp. 36–7.   [4] Potter, p. 35.   [5] *Ibid.*, p. 35.

With Chesterton bent on establishing that Catholics are humorous and Calvinists only witty, it seems that Potter's verdict is less arbitrary. Though wit predominates there is probably, by virtue of one or more of its many definitions, humour in every Shaw play. To quote but a few examples, there is the humour of acquiescence or acceptance in *Man and Superman* with the discomfiture of Tanner, the man of wit, when he capitulates to the biological urge which he himself attacks. He is certainly not overthrown by wit. There is humour in *Captain Brassbound's Conversion* with the narrow escape of the realist, Lady Cicely, from marrying Brassbound. There is humour in the defeat of Valentine, the Duellist of Sex, in *You Never Can Tell*. There is humour in Richard Dudgeon's desertion to romanticism. It is the humour that has been noted in another context, the humour that springs from the realisation and acceptance of the inconsistency in man, the humour of seeing both sides of the question, the humour that delights in puncturing displays of superiority so often expressed in the form of wit, that delights in laughing at those who spend their time laughing at others, that prefers to champion orthodoxy against unorthodoxy.

Moreover, in the examples given, it will be seen that yet another of the characteristics of humour, that of self-analysis and self-criticism, is present; for Shaw is laughing at his own realism. It is, indeed, a reversion to introversion; and we should therefore expect greater recourse to humour in those plays in which there is an element of tragic despair, where Shaw is finding it difficult to accept the validity of his own extroverted philosophy, or, in other words, to take himself seriously. Consequently, whereas the tone of, say, *Man and Superman*, is witty, that of *John Bull's Other Island* is humorous. The main source of fun in the latter play is derived from Broadbent. Shaw laughs at his inconsistencies and intellectual frailty, but he remains a hero. Despite his stupidity, Broadbent endears himself to the audience, whereas Roebuck Ramsden in *Man and Superman* arouses something near to contempt:

RAMSDEN (*touched on his most sensitive point*). I deny that. I will not allow you or any man to treat me as if I were a mere member of the British public. I detest its prejudices; I scorn its narrowness; I demand the right to think for myself. You pose as an advanced man. Let me tell you that I was an advanced man before you were born.

TANNER. I knew it was a long time ago.

RAMSDEN. I am as advanced as ever I was. I defy you to prove that I have ever hauled down the flag. I am more advanced than ever I was. I grow more advanced every day.

TANNER. More advanced in years, Polonius.

Man and Superman, Act I, p. 337.

Throughout the play Ramsden is a vulnerable and irascible target for wit, but Broadbent remains almost imperturbable and comes through unscathed. Doyle often loses his temper with Keegan but Broadbent remains naïvely anxious to understand his point of view:

BROADBENT (*seriously*). Too true, Mr Keegan, only too true. And most eloquently put. It reminds me of poor Ruskin: a great man, you know. I sympathize. Believe me, I'm on your side. Dont sneer, Larry: I used to read a lot of Shelley years ago. Let us be faithful to the dreams of our youth (*he wafts a wreath of cigar smoke at large across the hill*).

John Bull's Other Island, Act IV, pp. 450–1.

In *Major Barbara*, too, the tone of the play is witty and not humorous. But, as already noted, humour plays a significant part in avoiding tragic implications. It is the medium through which Cusins is brought to accept the tragic inconsistencies of a life in which theories do not fit the facts, to accept Undershaftism as a workable philosophy. Cusins's conversion is scarcely a triumph for wit. As he himself says later on, 'Mr Undershaft: you are, as far as I am able to gather, a most infernal old rascal; but you appeal very strongly to my sense of ironic humour'.[6] Ironic withdrawal or acceptance are characteristic of both tragedy and humour.

In *Heartbreak House*, this combination is pushed to its paradoxical extreme in a play of complete acceptance and despair. Both Barbara and Keegan are qualified in their acquiescence. But in *Heartbreak House*, acquiescence is so complete that nothing but desolation remains. Although there are witty characters, such as Lady Utterword, there is no dominating witty realist; for the choice is no longer between realism and romance but between different kinds of romance. The cocksureness of wit has gone, the characters wallowing in an irresolution

---

[6] *Major Barbara*, Act II, p. 479.

which is both humorous and tragic. The wit technique of heartlessness finally develops into the grim humour of the grave:

> *A terrific explosion shakes the earth. They reel back into their seats, or clutch the nearest support. They hear the falling of the shattered glass from the windows.*
>
> MAZZINI. Is anyone hurt?
>
> HECTOR. Where did it fall?
>
> NURSE GUINNESS (*in hideous triumph*). Right in the gravel pit: I seen it. Serve un right! I seen it. (*She runs away towards the gravel pit, laughing harshly.*)
>
> HECTOR. One husband gone.
>
> CAPTAIN SHOTOVER. Thirty pounds of good dynamite wasted.
>
> MAZZINI. Oh, poor Mangan!
>
> HECTOR. Are you immortal that you need pity him? Our turn next.
>
> *They wait in silence and intense expectation. Hesione and Ellie hold each other's hand tight.*
>
> *A distant explosion is heard.*
>
> MRS HUSHABYE (*relaxing her grip*). Oh! they have passed us.
>
> LADY UTTERWORD. The danger is over, Randall. Go to bed.
>
> CAPTAIN SHOTOVER. Turn in, all hands. The ship is safe. (*He sits down and goes asleep.*)
>
> ELLIE (*disappointedly*). Safe!
>
> HECTOR (*disgustedly*). Yes, safe. And how damnably dull the world has become again suddenly! (*He sits down.*)
>
> *Heartbreak House*, Act III, p. 802.

There is, however, an alternative to such extreme withdrawal, the key to which is to be found in the character of Shotover.

3. MADNESS

Tragedy and humour unite yet again in the portrayal of madness and near madness. It is probably no more possible to analyse madness into its tragic and humorous components than it is to make an exact distinction between wit and humour. There has been some refinement of taste since a little over a century ago when the antics of the madman

were a popular public spectacle; but perhaps this refinement is in part
the result of a heightened sense of the tragic in a less confident world,
the decline of tragedy, with its well-defined moral values, as a literary
form being merely another reflection of this loss of confidence. William
Blake has come into his own; and since the failure of extroverted
sanity to save the world, more and more attention is paid to the 'insanity' of the mystic and madman. The element of truth in wit has
already been discussed, and madness is yet another form of humour in
which the truth is served up in an unexpected form. Bergson recog-
nises the element of truth in some forms of madness: "If there exists
a madness that is laughable, it can only be one compatible with the
general health of the mind,—a sane type of madness, one might say."[7]
But his 'general health of the mind' is a very loose criterion and is only
useful in precluding the extremities of madness which arouse pity and
horror. It might be more accurate to say that madness can be laughable
if it contains some revelation of the truth. In Shaw, this alliance between
truth and disordered wits grows stronger as he grows older. By the
time he wrote *Man and Superman*, the vehicle for the truth is no longer
to be found in the sober sanity of Bluntschli in *Arms and the Man* and
of Caesar in *Caesar and Cleopatra*, but in the feverish dogmatism of
Tanner who is described in the stage directions as 'possibly a little mad'
and as 'a megalomaniac, who would be lost without a sense of humour'.[8] In *John Bull's Other Island*, it is Keegan, considered by the Church
as 'a poor madman, unfit and unworthy to take charge of the souls of
the people',[9] who has a vision of the ultimate truth which he presents
with no small wit. And it is Broadbent, whose naïvety is the main
source of humour, who has the greatest grasp of immediate reality. In
Major Barbara, it is Barbara in a semi-mystical strain who really has the
last word. She can be looked upon as a sophisticated forerunner of Saint
Joan, a simple peasant girl whose wisdom is greater than that of her
erudite opponents. Shotover in *Heartbreak House*, too, may be mad,
but he is not stupid.

On occasion Shaw alludes to the truth to be found in madness by
ironically calling his own sanity into question:

I am in the further difficulty that I have not yet ascertained the
truth about myself. For instance, how far am I mad, and how far sane?

[7] Bergson, p. 186.   [8] *Man and Superman*, Act I, p. 335.
[9] *John Bull's Other Island*, Act II, p. 417.

I do not know. My specific talent has enabled me to cut a figure in my profession in London; but a man may, like Don Quixote, be clever enough to cut a figure, and yet be stark mad.

He adds, however, a further comment on his insanity:

In the Mexican War, the Americans burnt the Spanish fleet, and finally had to drag wounded men out of hulls which had become furnaces. The effect of this on one of the American commanders was to make him assemble his men and tell them that he wished to declare before them that he believed in God Almighty. . . . On reading it, and observing that the newspapers, representing normal public opinion, seemed to consider it a very creditable, natural, and impressively pious incident, I came to the conclusion that I must be mad. At all events, if I am sane, the rest of the world ought not to be at large. We cannot both see things as they really are.

Sixteen Self Sketches, No. VIII, p. 43.

But madness for Shaw was not just an ironic means for the revelation of the truth. The not infrequent union of tragedy, which treats of the powerlessness of action, and humour, with its acceptance of the *status quo*, represents a contempt and evasion of what Caesar, a most thoughgoing realist, himself called "this tedious, brutal life of action!".[10] Madness provided not only an ironic commentary but also a means of escaping the mental paralysis which, in the form of an all-pervasive irony, lies in wait for the inveterate maker of wit. It is both protective and catalytic. It rejects extroversion but attempts to make introversion bearable and constructive. Shotover's 'seventh degree of concentration' is constructive in so far as it is an affirmation of faith that salvation will be achieved in the realm of mind and not of action. A crazy affirmation it may be, but it is made respectable in the doctrine of Creative Evolution. An external God and external action having failed, Man becomes God and an inner Nirvana is to be sought through a concentration of the will. Quoted already in another context are Keegan's last words:

In my dreams it is a country where the State is the Church and the Church the people: three in one and one in three. It is a common-

---

[10] *Caesar and Cleopatra*, Act IV., p. 286.

wealth in which work is play and play is life: three in one and one in
three. It is a temple in which the priest is the worshipper and the
worshipper the worshipped: three in one and one in three. It is a
godhead in which all life is human and all humanity divine: three
in one and one in three. It is, in short, the dream of a madman.

John Bull's Other Island, Act IV, p. 452.

And the 'dream of a madman' comes to theoretical fruition in *Back
to Methuselah* when the self becomes the final reality:

THE HE-ANCIENT. And I, like Acis, ceased to walk over the mountains with my friends, and walked alone; for I found that I had
creative power over myself but none over my friends. And then I
ceased to walk on the mountains; for I saw that the mountains were
dead.

. . . . . .

THE SHE-ANCIENT. . . . When I discarded my dolls as he discarded
his friends and his mountains, it was to myself I turned as to the
final reality. Here, and here alone, I could shape and create. When
my arm was weak and I willed it to be strong, I could create a roll
of muscle on it; and when I understood that, I understood that I
could without any greater miracle give myself ten arms and three
heads.

THE HE-ANCIENT. I also came to understand such miracles. For
fifty years I sat contemplating this power in myself and concentrating
my will.

Back to Methuselah, Part V, pp. 957–8.

And like Vivie Warren in *Mrs Warren's Profession*, Martellus forsook
the company of the opposite sex to study Mathematics.[11] From the
introverted sanity of the world-renouncer, Vivie Warren, through the
mad Keegan's identification of worshipper and worshipped, through
mad Shotover's 'seventh degree of concentration' to the sanity of the
Ancients with their renunciation of the senses and the external world,
the path is clear. Transfiguration and final apotheosis through madness.
The irony that ends irony.

But, however imposing the philosophical robes, they do not cover,

[11] *Back to Methuselah*, Pt. V, p. 960.

K

nor were they intended to cover, Shaw's failure to come to immediate terms with life:

> HECTOR. What is the dynamite for?
>
> CAPTAIN SHOTOVER. To kill fellows like Mangan.
>
> HECTOR. No use. They will always be able to buy more dynamite than you.
>
> CAPTAIN SHOTOVER. I will make a dynamite that he cannot explode.
>
> HECTOR. And that you can, eh?
>
> CAPTAIN SHOTOVER. Yes: when I have attained the seventh degree of concentration.
>
> HECTOR. Whats the use of that? You never do attain it.
>
> CAPTAIN SHOTOVER. What then is to be done? Are we to be kept for ever in the mud by these hogs to whom the universe is nothing but a machine for greasing their bristles and filling their snouts?
>
> HECTOR. Are Mangan's bristles worse than Randall's lovelocks?
>
> CAPTAIN SHOTOVER. We must win powers of life and death over them both. I refuse to die until I have invented the means.
>
> *Heartbreak House*, Act I, p. 773.

Shotover may refuse to die, but the era of the long-livers of *Back to Methuselah* is not yet, and his refusal is merely a symptom, not of constructive, but of self-protective madness. He is, however, less mad than Mangan who is sane. He is not even mad enough for his own comfort. 'Give me', he cries, 'deeper darkness. Money is not made in the light.'[12] As Lucas says, 'Sophocles and Meredith indeed have both expressed the view—doubtless in moments of spleen—that it is happier to be an idiot. But they were thinking of a blissfully complete idiocy which is beyond the reach of most of us.'[13] Nevertheless, even if it is beyond the reach of Shotover-Shaw, the mere simulation of idiocy acted as a palliative. Far more significant impersonations of Shaw than the trumpet-tongued realists are to be found in Keegan and Shotover; for the realists were mainly mouthpieces for his ideas whereas the two 'madmen' are more artistic projections of self, the self who pretended to wonder 'how far am I mad, and how far sane?' In madness some integration of the personality could be achieved by lessening the dis-

---

[12] *Heartbreak House*, Act I, p. 775.
[13] F. L. Lucas, *Literature and Psychology*, 1951, p. 217.

parity between the real and the ideal. The 'slightly mad' Tanner bridged the gap by the megalomaniacal intensity of his attack. The melancholy Keegan found relief in talking to a grasshopper and, as did Hamlet, in an affirmation of his own madness; while at the height of Shaw's despair a very thick crust of eccentricity overlays Shotover's sanity, which writhes in torment underneath. Humour and tragedy are both there, the self-analysis, self-depreciation, and diffidence of humour being pushed to tragic extremes and constituting a partial substitution of a dream world for the real world.

But Shaw's ventures into madness are short-lived; for, as Bentley says, Shaw 'never relaxed into self-pity'.[14] There is in Keegan and Shotover the pathos to be found in the highest flights of humour; but both retain the belligerence of wit, usually expressing themselves in a language which has none of the gentleness and obliquity of humour or the obfuscation of madness. And for the great majority of plays, both before and after *Heartbreak House*, Bentley is right when he says that it was Shaw's 'celebrated gaiety' that served as 'a prophylactic against such relaxation'.[15] Nevertheless, Shaw was in despair, and the gaiety, being a prophylactic rather than an integral part of his artistic expression, very frequently found vent, not in an organic wit, but in a parasitic flippancy which has so bewildered even sympathetic critics. His answer to a crazy inconsequential world is not usually to be found in tragedy or pathos but in an inconsequential craziness. Withdrawal may take many forms; and, in the twentieth century, from Karl Marx to Groucho Marx is not such a long step.

4. FLIPPANCY

It is in two extensive periods, the first between *Major Barbara* and *Heartbreak House* and the second after *Saint Joan*, that this flippancy is most in evidence. It was another defence against despair and frustration, a withdrawal from a conflict that could not be resolved. For just as the intrusion of the values of comedy into tragedy constitute a withdrawal and a false catharsis, so does flippancy imply some measure of withdrawal from even the more immediate purposes of comedy. The transposition of key is so extreme that the purposive element in wit is entirely or partially eliminated, or else is lost from sight under a superimposed layer of clowning for clowning's sake; while the acquiescence

---

[14] Bentley, *Shaw*, p. 229.   [15] *Ibid.*, p. 229.

K*

and self-identification of humour give way to apparent indifference and non-participation. It is the loudest and, at the same time, the most detached and implicit form of irony. The very inextinguishability of the laughter of the gods is evidence of their detachment and flippancy.

But the phenomenon of flippancy is, of course, another aspect of the interaction of technique and outlook. The successful wit technique has taken the technician captive and developed into an eccentricity. Perhaps some eccentricity is inevitable in anybody who spends his life writing. It is almost impossible to maintain an attitude or an emotion at its original strength, and eccentricity of style develops when there is no longer an urgent need of expression. During the periods under discussion, and particularly during the later period, Shaw no longer felt this need. He had said it all so many times before. He no longer believed in the educability of man, in the possibility of effecting conversion. He experienced the weariness that comes to all reformers who spend their lives butting their heads against a wall of apathy, stupidity, and moral insensibility. It is not accidental that the plays in which flippancy is most abundant are the plays which display little dramatic force. In the later period this is almost certainly due in part to a decline in creative power, so that farcical expedients become a means of holding the attention of the audience. But a decline in creative power is an insufficient explanation; for flippancy showed itself before such great plays as *Pygmalion*, *Heartbreak House*, and *Saint Joan* were written. It was an expression of the irritability, impatience, and contempt, which were the outcome of his loss of faith in the power of objectivity. In the polemics it sometimes led to irresponsibility of utterance, and in the plays to a loss of verisimilitude. Social comedy gave way to extravaganza. Situations were arbitrarily manipulated and divorced from probability. Characters were capriciously handled and insufficiently motivated. Antagonists degenerated into defenceless Aunt Sallies, the lack of conflict accentuating a didacticism which, in its turn, sought mitigation in still more flippancy. That Shaw's comedic talents remained practically unimpaired after his dramatic and doctrinal force had deteriorated merely accentuated these characteristics.

The arbitrary manipulation of plot usually admits the attributes of farce, with its coincidences, extravagant characterisations, and physical contrivances, designed almost entirely to raise laughter. Not that Shaw, except in a few one-act tomfooleries, ever wrote pure farce. But although there is nearly always a serious purpose, the disproportion between matter and comic device often places a play on a farcical level. During the period preceding *Heartbreak House*, the most significant example from the point of Shaw's development is to be found in *Misalliance* (1910).

Misalliance purports to deal with the relation of parents and children; but its theme, if it has one at all, seems to be similar to that of *Heartbreak House*. Both plays treat of futility and the paralysis of action. Hypatia is Ellie, waiting for something to happen. 'They never do anything: they only discuss whether what other people do is right.'[16] It is true that in *Heartbreak House* there is a silly burglar *ex machina*, who finds that he has broken into the home of Shotover, his old sea-captain; but apart from this idiotic coincidence, a realistic tableau is built up and the conflict of ideas which has brought about the paralysis of action is set forth with just as much cogency and clarity as is consistent with the necessary atmosphere of indecision and eccentricity. The development of disillusion in Ellie and the deterioration of Mangan and others are skilfully unfolded, with Shotover's increasing sanity and Hector's increasing seriousness supplying the counterpoint. In *Misalliance*, however, the theme is lost beneath a continuous stream of silliness and what Potts calls 'physical sensationalism'.[17] There is the irruption of Gunner who has come to shoot Tarleton for betraying his mother thirty years previously. There is the shattering arrival in a crashed aeroplane of Percival, who, strangely enough, is already known to the household. With him is Lina Szcezepanowska, who appears to be a man but turns out to be a woman. She is an acrobat, one of Shaw's long, dreary, farcical line of beautiful but physically powerful women. Consisting in great part of almost disconnected dialogues, a further symptom of weak construction, the play abounds in such physical buffooneries. Hypatia, who is apparently determined to make something happen, chases Percival. He in turn chases Hypatia. Johnny nearly hits Bentley. Tarleton dissolves into out-of-character tears. Bentley throws tantrums and, in mortal fear, is finally led off to take an aeroplane trip by Lina. At the end, Hypatia's 'Thank Goodness!' in reply to Tarleton's 'Well, I suppose—er—I suppose theres nothing more to be said'[18] is presumably an attempt to resurrect a theme which has never been born.

Such physical sensationalism is a commonplace in many other plays, and is by no means confined to the violence which is the familiar

[16] *Misalliance*, p. 626.   [17] Potts, p. 151.   [18] *Misalliance*, p. 644.

obbligato to Shavian love affairs. The first scene of the Prologue to *The Simpleton of the Unexpected Isles* ends with a comic suicide, the second scene with the Emigration Officer being kicked into the bay, and the third scene with the Young Woman being thrown into the bay. In Act I, a comic clergyman is put ashore on a tropical island by a gang of pirates who have kidnapped him from Weston-super-Mare to lend a deceptive respectability to their enterprises. In Act II the angel arrives, shaking from his wings and clothes the bullets and small shot of which he has been the target.

To this flippant farrago of violence and sudden death, with the wit of callous understatement pushed to a wearisome extreme, can be added Shaw's tedious preoccupation with farcical and often irrelevant love affairs, precipitous courtships, and sexless sexy talk, which are used to spice the dialogue and supply the plays with a superficial liveliness. People fall in unprovoked love, and propose unmotivated matrimony or motivated sex relations within a few minutes of meeting. But taboo wit, too, can become a mere mannerism and lose its effect with excessive use. Nudists do not laugh at each other.

Illustration by quotation is not effective, for most individual examples, written with the usual Shavian *élan*, are amusing enough. Quotations from *Buoyant Billions* to show that satiety can be reached within forty or fifty lines would not be in the interests of criticism, for he wrote the play at the age of 91. His previous play, '*In Good King Charles's Golden Days*', written at the age of 83, is a rollicking conversation-piece almost in Shaw's best manner.

The arbitrary manipulation of plot inevitably entails the elimination of genuine conflict. In the great plays it is the conflict which provides movement, tempo, and solidity. But when Shaw loses his faith in the betterment of the human race through the force of reason, there is no longer any purpose in depicting the struggle between rationality and irrationality. The irrational is now dismissed with such contempt that it is not even felt to be necessary to present the rational with care and cogency. In *Too True to Be Good*, for example, there is no conflict except on the level of farcical action. Ideas are communicated through preaching, not pleading.

The principal character is Aubrey:

AUBREY. Most likely. But I am a born preacher, not a pleader. The theory of legal procedure is that if you set two liars to expose one another, the truth will emerge. That would not suit me. I greatly dislike being contradicted; and the only place where a man is safe from contradiction is in the pulpit. I detest argument: it is unmannerly, and obscures the preacher's message. Besides, the law is too much concerned with crude facts and too little with spiritual things; and it is in spiritual things that I am interested: they alone call my gift into full play.

Too True to be Good, Act II, p. 1146.

AUBREY. . . . . Nature never intended me for soldiering or thieving: I am by nature and destiny a preacher. I am the new Ecclesiastes. But I have no Bible, no creed: the war has shot both out of my hands. The war has been a fiery forcing house in which we have grown with a rush like flowers in a late spring following a terrible winter. And with what result? This: that we have outgrown our religion, outgrown our political system, outgrown our own strength of mind and character. The fatal word NOT has been miraculously inserted into all our creeds: in the desecrated temples where we knelt murmuring 'I believe' we stand with stiff knees and stiffer necks shouting 'Up, all! the erect posture is the mark of the man: let lesser creatures kneel and crawl: we will not kneel and we do not believe.' But what next? Is NO enough? For a boy, yes: for a man, never. Are we any the less obsessed with a belief when we are denying it than when we were affirming it? No: I must have affirmations to preach. Without them the young will not listen to me; for even the young grow tired of denials. The negative-monger falls before the soldiers, the men of action, the fighters, strong in the old uncompromising affirmations which give them status, duties, certainty of consequences; so that the pugnacious spirit of man in them can reach out and strike deathblows with steadfastly closed minds. Their way is straight and sure; but it is the way of death; and the preacher must preach the way of life. Oh, if I could only find it! (*A white sea fog swirls up from the beach to his feet, rising and thickening round him.*) I am ignorant: I have lost my nerve and am intimidated: all I know is that I must find the way of life, for myself and all of us, or we shall surely perish. And meanwhile my gift has possession of me: I must preach and preach and preach no matter how late the hour and how short the day, no matter whether I have nothing to say. . . .

Ibid., Act III, p. 1167.

This is Shaw writing his own epilogue at the end of a play in which all the characters are without creed, and in which he hardly makes a single affirmation to which denial can be made. As a result, farce is piled on farce—successful farce, too, for this is one of the funniest plays Shaw ever wrote. That all the other characters fled when the farce was over and Aubrey started his peroration provides, perhaps, the best of all exemplifications on the function of flippancy in Shaw.

There are, of course, minor points of conflict on matters of importance in the flippant plays; but they are seldom part of any integrating theme and they are all resolved by a mere wave of some dialectical wand or by some farcical manoeuvre. In *Getting Married*, which might be looked upon as the spiritual forerunner of all the flippant plays, the main point at issue, to which little attention is given, turns on the refusal of a young couple to marry each other because they have suddenly realised the legal implications of such a step. This 'conflict' is resolved as follows:

> LESBIA. You have both given in, have you?
>
> EDITH. Not at all. We have provided for everything.
>
> SOAMES. How?
>
> EDITH. Before going to the church, we went to the office of that insurance company—whats its name, Cecil?
>
> SYKES. The British Family Insurance Corporation. It insures you against poor relations and all sorts of family contingencies.
>
> EDITH. It has consented to insure Cecil against libel actions brought against him on my account. It will give us specially low terms because I am a Bishop's daughter.
>
> SYKES. And I have given Edie my solemn word that if I ever commit a crime I'll knock her down before a witness and go off to Brighton with another lady.
>
> *Getting Married*, p. 584.

Such flippant conversions and motivations abound. In *Too True to be Good*, Mrs Mopply is converted by being struck over the head with an umbrella. In *On the Rocks*, Sir Arthur is converted to Socialism between Acts I and II after a stay in a health retreat. In *The Millionairess*, the Doctor, a comparatively serious character for such a play, is converted to matrimony by the quality of the lady's pulse. In *Androcles and the Lion*, the Emperor is won over to the side of the Christians by the feats of Ferrovius, and to the truth of Christianity by the lion's refusal to eat Androcles. In *Fanny's First Play*, the conflict between parents and children is swept away in the tradition of drawing-room farce by a double marriage, one between the son and his prostitute and the other between the daughter and a butler who turns out to be a duke. In *The Simpleton of the Unexpected Isles*, the parasites are exterminated by an act of God. Even *On the Rocks*, which, re-enacting as it does Shaw's frustrated socialist aspirations, treats the main conflict with some seriousness, contains another farcical double marriage which sets Sir Arthur free to go and live in a 'cottage near a good golf links. . . .'[19]

This lack of genuine conflict entails stupid antagonists who are not worth anything but flippant treatment by the protagonists. Caricatures, which in the great plays occupied only minor roles such as accorded Britannus in *Caesar and Cleopatra* and the Chaplain in *Saint Joan*, now become major characters. The actual simpleton of the Unexpected Isles is a feeble-minded clergyman called Iddy, which is short for idiot. In *Fanny's First Play*, the mother and the father are naïve in their bewilderment. In *Too True To Be Good*, Mrs Mopply is a frantically silly exponent of orthodox medicine. In *Misalliance*, Gunner is crudely contemptible as a socialist. In *The Apple Cart*, Boanerges is wildly egregious as a Man of the People. In *Geneva*, the Bishop is an impossibly insulated nincompoop, Begonia is a female Colonel Blimp, and the Widow is an anti-Semite of puerile ignorance and prejudice. Together with other aspects of his art, Shaw lost interest in his characters. He no longer bothers to describe or explain them at any length in the stage directions and, in frequently providing them with silly unreal names, descends to one of the most pitiful forms of humour.

The more obvious didacticism, which inevitably accompanied the elimination of conflict, necessitated even further injections of flippancy. The wit becomes more and more callous and more and more defiant of taboo, not only to make violence and sudden death comic, but also to moderate the moral tone—to which he had temporarily reverted in *Heartbreak House*. Shaw compensates for the abandonment of comedy in favour of satiric over-emphasis by a plethora of extravagantly comic device. Now satiric over-emphasis, which is another name for didacticism, is more evident in allegory than in any other literary form; and, in later life, Shaw's plays tended to become more and more allegorical in form and method. And, significantly enough, where the use of allegorical characteristics is most obvious, so is the element of flippancy.

[19] *On the Rocks*, p. 1218.

In the most farcical part of *Androcles and the Lion*, the allegorical element is so pronounced that even a lion is endowed with human qualities. In *The Simpleton of the Unexpected Isles*, the arrival of the angel provides a farcical highlight. In the riotous Prologue to *Too True to be Good*, a bloated bacillus personifies commonsense nature treatment as opposed to orthodox medicine. What, too, is the notoriously flippant Epilogue to *Saint Joan* but allegory? *Back to Methuselah*, also allegorical in form, is perhaps a partial exception. But this play was written, according to Shaw, in a deliberately serious vein as an exposition of Creative Evolution. In writing about the Hell Scene in *Man and Superman*, he says:

> Accordingly, in 1901, I took the legend of Don Juan in its Mozartian form and made it a dramatic parable of Creative Evolution. But being then at the height of my invention and comedic talent, I decorated it too brilliantly and lavishly. I surrounded it with a comedy of which it formed only one act . . . The effect was so vertiginous, apparently, that nobody noticed the new religion in the centre of the intellectual whirlpool . . . I now find myself inspired to make a second legend of Creative Evolution without distractions and embellishments. My sands are running out; the exuberance of 1901 has aged into the garrulity of 1920; and the war has been a stern intimation that the matter is not one to be trifled with.
>
> *Back to Methuselah*, Prefaces, pp. 523-4.

Being Shaw, he could not entirely refrain from 'distractions and embellishments', but compared to nearly all the later plays it is free from extraneous flippancies and farcical expedients with the result that, although dialectical ingenuity and Shavian verve save even Parts I and V, the most highly allegorical sections, from being dull in the reading, the play as a whole is not dramatically successful. The doctrine that he seeks to teach is presented too directly and the characters are mere caricatures in so far as they are not even types but the embodiment of ideas. However, in *Back to Methuselah*, this failure to retain an essential sense of metaphor is not disastrous, for the idea of Creative Evolution was sufficiently novel. But when the idea was as banal as, say, that people without function should be eliminated, as in *The Simpleton of the Unexpected Isles*, then it needed all the frivolity at Shaw's command to pass muster. Dull or monotonous fare needs to be highly seasoned.

Despite, then, failing powers, the growth of disillusionment, and a decline in dialectical content, all of which contributed to the transformation of rhetorical ornament into farcical virtuosity, Shaw remained an artist to the end. Theoretically he was Platonic in his rejection of art for truth. But in spite of his claim that he wrote plays with no other incentive but conversion,[20] he knew that he wrote for other reasons. Indeed, he knew that his wit often obscured his message. He would have agreed with Professor Ifor Evans that 'Shaw's message would have been clearer if the wit had been less',[21] and with Edmund Wilson who said that '—all the qualities that have had the effect of weakening his work as a publicist—have contributed to his success as an artist'.[22] His remarks on the limitations of *Man and Superman* as a vehicle for the propounding of Creative Evolution have already been quoted. Of *Arms and the Man* he wrote: 'I had the curious experience of witnessing an apparently insane success, with the actors and actresses almost losing their heads with the intoxication of laugh after laugh, and of going before the curtain to tremendous applause, the only person in the theatre who knew that the whole affair was a ghastly failure.'[23] It may well be, despite T. S. Eliot's opinion that comedy is a better vehicle than tragedy for serious statement, that although wit makes such an instantaneous impact, it is of little use for permanent conversion. Spinoza said that the only way of eliminating one emotion is by substituting another; and wit with its intellectual approach is not fitted for such a task. Rousseau had more influence than Voltaire, Luther than Erasmus, Harriet Beecher Stowe than Mark Twain, Wesley and Wilberforce than Swift and Fielding. Perhaps laughter provokes a feeling, not of guilt, but of superiority. Perhaps it relaxes tension to the point of indifference. And perhaps, as Swift says, 'Satyr is a sort of *Glass*, wherein beholders do generally discover every body's Face but their Own.'[24] But none of these strictures on the efficacy of wit as a means of conversion is relevant as criticism of a playwright the worst of whose plays are redeemed by a comic sense unsurpassed in English literature.

[20] *The Shewing-up of Blanco Posnet*, Prefaces, p. 409.
[21] Quoted by Maurice Colbourne, *The Real Bernard Shaw*, 1949, p. 253.
[22] Wilson, *Triple Thinkers*, p. 171.
[23] *The Life and Letters of Henry Arthur Jones*, ed. Doris Arthur Jones, 1930, pp. 140–41; quoted by Alick West, *A Good Man Fallen Among Fabians*, 1950, p. 82.
[24] Jonathan Swift, *The Battle of the Books*, Preface, *The Prose Works of Jonathan Swift*, ed. Herbert Davis, 1939, p. 140.

Works Mentioned in this Book

1. TEXTS

A. *Plays*

SHAW, Bernard. *The Complete Plays of Bernard Shaw*, Munksgaard, Copenhagen, by arrangement with Odhams Press, London, n.d. (This edition is identical with the edition published in 1934 by Odhams Press, London, which does not include plays written after *On the Rocks* (1933). A complete list of plays and novels and the date of composition is given in the Appendix.)

B. *Novels*

SHAW, Bernard. *Cashel Byron's Profession* (1882), Constable (standard edition), London, 1950.

SHAW, Bernard. *An Unsocial Socialist* (1883), Constable (standard edition), London, 1950.

C. *Prefaces*

SHAW, Bernard. *Prefaces by Bernard Shaw*, Constable, London, 1934.

D. *Political and Occasional*

SHAW, Bernard. *Everybody's Political What's What?*, Constable, London, 1944.

SHAW, Bernard. *The Intelligent Woman's Guide to Socialism, Capitalism, Sovietism, and Fascism*, 2 vols., Penguin, London, 1937. Originally published under the title of *The Intelligent Woman's Guide to Socialism and Capitalism*, Constable, London, 1928. (The Pelican edition, which contains two additional chapters, is preferred, as the 'Author's Note' contains a statement on his later political views.)

SHAW, Bernard. *Major Critical Essays:* 'The Quintessence of Ibsenism' (1891), 'The Perfect Wagnerite' (1898), 'The Sanity of Art' (1895), Constable (standard edition), London, 1947.

SHAW, Bernard. *Pen Portraits and Reviews*, Constable (standard edition), London, 1949.

SHAW, Bernard. *Sixteen Self Sketches*, Constable (standard edition), London, 1949.

2. BIOGRAPHICAL AND CRITICAL

ARCHER, William. *The Old Drama and the New: An Essay in Re-valuation*, Heinemann, London, 1923.

ARISTOTLE. *Poetics, etc.*, Everyman edition, Dent, London, 1949. (Includes A Digest of Aristotle's *Rhetoric* by Thomas Hobbes.)

BENTLEY, Eric. *Bernard Shaw*, Robert Hale, London, 1950.

BENTLEY, Eric. *The Modern Theatre: A Study of Dramatists and Drama*, Robert Hale, London, 1948.

BERGSON, Henri. *Laughter: An Essay on the Meaning of the Comic*, tr. by C. Brereton and F. Rothwell, Macmillan, London, 1911.

CHESTERTON, G. K. *George Bernard Shaw* (1909, with additional chapter, 1935), The Bodley Head, London, 1948.

COLBOURNE, Maurice. *The Real Bernard Shaw*, Dent, London, 1949.

EASTMAN, Max. *Enjoyment of Laughter*, Halcyon House, New York, 1936.

FREUD, Sigmund. *Wit and its Relation to the Unconscious* (1905), tr. by A. A. Brill, Kegan Paul, Trench, Trubner, London, 1922.

GOODMAN, Paul. *The Structure of Literature*, University of Chicago Press, Chicago, 1954.

HARRIS, Frank. *Bernard Shaw*, Gollancz, London, 1931.

IRVINE, William. The Universe of G.B.S., Whittlesey House, New York, 1949.

JOAD, C. E. M. *Shaw*, Gollancz, London, 1949.

JOAD, C. E. M. editor. *Shaw and Society: An Anthology and a Symposium*, Odhams, London, 1953.

KANT, Emmanuel. *Critique of Aesthetic Judgment*, tr. by James Creed Meredith, Oxford University Press, London, 1911.

KINGSMILL, Hugh. *The Progress of a Biographer*, Methuen, London, 1949.

KOESTLER, Arthur. *Insight and Outlook*, Macmillan, London, 1949.

KOESTLER, Arthur. *The Act of Creation*, Hutchinson, London, 1964.

LEYBURN, Ellen Douglass. *Satiric Allegory: Mirror of Man*, Yale University Press, New Haven, 1956.

LUCAS, F. L. *Literature and Psychology*, Cassell, London, 1951.

LUCAS, F. L. *Style*, Cassell, London, 1951.

MEREDITH, George. *An Essay on Comedy and the Uses of the Comic Spirit*, Archibald Constable, London, 1903.

MUGGERIDGE, Malcolm. Foreword, *Pick of Punch*, edited by Nicolas Bentley, Andre Deutsch, 1956.

MURRY, J. Middleton. *The Problem of Style*, Oxford University Press, London, 1922.

NETHERCOT, Arthur H. *Men and Supermen*, Harvard University Press, Cambridge (Massachusetts), 1954.

NICOLL, Allardyce. *An Introduction to Dramatic Theory*, Harrap, London, 1923.

NIETZSCHE, Friedrich. *The Philosophy of Nietzsche*, The Modern Library, New York, 1954.

PATCH, Blanche. *Thirty Years with G.B.S.*, Gollancz, London, 1951.

POTTER, Stephen. *Sense of Humour*, Max Reinhardt, London, 1954.

POTTS, L. J. *Comedy*, Hutchinson, London, 1948.

READ, Herbert. *English Prose Style*, Bell, London, 1928.

RICHARDS, I. A. *The Philosophy of Rhetoric*, Oxford University Press, New York, 1936.

RICHARDS, I. A. *Principles of Literary Criticism*, Routledge and Kegan Paul, London, 1924.

SCHLEGEL, A. W. *Lectures on Dramatic Art and Literature (1809–11)*, tr. John Black (1815), George Bell, London, 1892.

SCOTT-JAMES, R. A. *Fifty Years of English Literature*, 1900–1950, Longmans, Green, London, 1956.

SWIFT, Jonathan. *The Battle of the Books*, in *The Prose Works of Jonathan Swift*, Vol. I, edited by Herbert Davis, Shakespeare Head, Oxford, 1939.

TUVE, Rosemond. *Elizabethan and Metaphysical Imagery, Renaissance Poetic and Twentieth-century Critics*, University of Chicago Press, Chicago, 1947.

USSHER, Arland. *Three Great Irishmen*, Gollancz, London, 1952.

VULLIAMY, C. E., ed. *The Anatomy of Satire* (Preface), Michael Joseph, London, 1950.

WEST, Alick. *A Good Man Fallen Among Fabians*, Lawrence and Wishart, London, 1950.

WILSON, Edmund. 'Bernard Shaw on the Training of a Statesman' in *Classics and Commercials, A Literary Chronicle of the Forties*, W. H. Allen, London, 1951.

WILSON, Edmund. 'Bernard Shaw at Eighty' in *The Triple Thinkers, Twelve Essays on Literary Subjects*, John Lehmann, London, 1952.

WORCESTER, David. *The Art of Satire*, Harvard University Press, Cambridge (Massachusetts), 1940.

3. NEWSPAPERS AND PERIODICALS

TAYLOR, A. P. J. 'Shaw the Court Jester', *The Observer*, London, July 22, 1956.

PRITCHETT, V. S. 'The English Puritan', *New Statesman and Nation*, London, Jan. 26, 1957.

PRIESTLEY, J. B. 'Thoughts on Shaw', *New Statesman and Nation*, London, July 28, 1956.

Critical and Biographical Works also Consulted

BAIN, Alexander. *The Emotions and the Will* (3rd edition), Appleton, New York, 1876.

BENTLEY, Eric. *The Playwright as Thinker: A Study of Drama in Modern Times*, Harcourt, Brace, New York, 1946.

COLLIS, J. S. *Shaw*, Jonathan Cape, London, 1925.

COOPER, Lane. *An Aristotelian Theory of Comedy*, Harcourt, Brace, New York, 1922.

EASTMAN, Max. *The Sense of Humor*, Scribner, New York, 1921.

ERVINE, St. John. *Bernard Shaw: His Life, Work, and Friends*, Constable, London, 1956.

GREGORY, J. C. *The Nature of Laughter*, K. Paul, London, 1924.

GREIG, J. Y. T. *The Psychology of Laughter and Comedy*, George Allen and Unwin, London, 1923.

GROTJAHN, M. *Beyond Laughter*, McGraw, New York, 1957.

HENDERSON, Archibald. *Bernard Shaw, Playboy and Prophet*, Appleton, New York, 1932.

LUDOVICI, Antony. *The Secret of Laughter*, Constable, London, 1932.

KRONENBERGER, Louis, ed. *George Bernard Shaw*, World, Cleveland, 1953.

MEISEL, Martin. *Shaw and the Nineteenth-century Theater*, Princeton University Press, Princeton, 1963.

MENON, V. K. KRISHNA. *A Theory of Laughter, with Special Relation to Comedy and Tragedy*, George Allen and Unwin, London, 1931.

PEARSON, Hesketh. *Bernard Shaw: His Life and Personality*, Collins, London (new edn.), 1950.

RAPP, Albert. *The Origins of Wit and Humor*, Dutton, New York, 1951.

RATTRAY, R. F. *Bernard Shaw: A Chronicle*, Leagrove Press, Luton, 1951.

SIDIS, Boris. *The Psychology of Laughter*, Appleton, New York, 1913.

SULLY, JAMES. *An Essay on Laughter: Its Forms, its Causes, its Development and its Value*, Longmans, Green, London, 1902.

WARD, A. C. *Bernard Shaw*, Longmans, Green, London, 1951.

WILLIAMS, Raymond. *Drama from Ibsen to Eliot*, Chatto and Windus, London, 1952.

WINSTEN, Stephen. *Jesting Apostle: The Life of Bernard Shaw*, Hutchinson, London, 1956.

WINSTEN, Stephen, ed. *G.B.S. 90: Aspects of Bernard Shaw's Life and Works*, Hutchinson, London, 1946.

A Chronological List of the Plays and Novels of George Bernard Shaw

Novels

Date of Composition		Date of Composition	
1879	Immaturity	1882	Cashel Byron's Profession
1880	The Irrational Knot	1883	An Unsocial Socialist
1881	Love among the Artists		

Plays

1885–1892	Widowers' Houses	1910	Fanny's First Play
1893	The Philanderer	1911–1912	Androcles and the Lion
	Mrs Warren's Profession	1912	Pygmalion
1894	Arms and the Man		Overruled
	Candida	1913	Great Catherine
1895	The Man of Destiny		The Music Cure
1896	You Never Can Tell	1913–1919	Heartbreak House
	The Devil's Disciple	1916	O'Flaherty, V.C.
1898	Caesar and Cleopatra		The Inca of Perusalem
1899	Captain Brassbound's Conversion		Augustus Does His Bit
1901	The Admirable Bashville	1917	Annajanska, the Bolshevik Empress
1901–1903	Man and Superman	1918–1920	Back to Methuselah
1904	John Bull's Other Island	1923	Saint Joan
	How He lied to Her Husband	1929	The Apple Cart
		1931	Too True to be Good
1905	Major Barbara	1933	On the Rocks
	Passion, Poison, and Petrifaction		Village Wooing
		1934	The Six of Calais
1906	The Doctor's Dilemma		The Simpleton of the Unexpected Isles
1908	Getting Married		
1909	The Shewing-up of Blanco Posnet	1936	The Millionairess
		1937	Cymbeline Refinished
	The Fascinating Foundling	1938	Geneva
	Press Cuttings	1939	'In Good King Charles's Golden Days'
	A Glimpse of Reality	1946–1947	Buoyant Billions
1909–1910	Misalliance	1949	Farfetched Fables
1910	The Dark Lady of the Sonnets		Shakes versus Shav

Index

B50428

Mayne, Frederick.
　　The wit and satire of Bernard Shaw, by Fred Mayn⟨e⟩
New York, St. Martin's Press, 1967.

　　x, 154 p.　23 cm.

　　Bibliography: p. 146–149.

　　1. Shaw, George Bernard, 1856–1950.　ɪ. Title.

PR5368.W5M3　19⟨ ⟩　　822′.9′12　　67–1400⟨ ⟩